THE ROWMAN & LITTLEFIELD HANDBOOK FOR CRITICAL THINKING

THE ROWMAN & LITTLEFIELD HANDBOOK FOR CRITICAL THINKING

Noel Hendrickson, Kirk St. Amant, William Hawk, William O'Meara, and Daniel Flage

ROWMAN & LITTLEFIELD PUBLISHERS, INC.
Lanham • Boulder • New York • Toronto • Plymouth, UK

ROWMAN & LITTLEFIELD PUBLISHERS, INC.

Published in the United States of America
by Rowman & Littlefield Publishers, Inc.
A wholly owned subsidiary of The Rowman & Littlefield Publishing Group, Inc.
4501 Forbes Boulevard, Suite 200, Lanham, Maryland 20706
www.rowmanlittlefield.com

Estover Road
Plymouth PL6 7PY
United Kingdom

British Library Cataloguing in Publication Information Available

Library of Congress Cataloging-in-Publication Data:

The Rowman & Littlefield handbook for critical thinking / Noel Hendrickson . . .
[et al.].
    p. cm.
Includes bibliographical references (p.   ) and index.
ISBN-13: 978-0-7425-5978-3 (cloth : alk. paper)
ISBN-10: 0-7425-5978-5 (cloth : alk. paper)
ISBN-13: 978-0-7425-5979-0 (pbk. : alk. paper)
ISBN-10: 0-7425-5979-3 (pbk. : alk. paper)
    1. Critical thinking. I. Hendrickson, Noel, 1974– II. Rowman and Littlefield, Inc.
III. Title: Rowman and Littlefield handbook for critical thinking. IV. Title: Handbook
for critical thinking.
    BF441.R69 2008
    160—dc22   2007037764

Printed in the United States of America

♾™ The paper used in this publication meets the minimum requirements of
American National Standard for Information Sciences—Permanence of Paper
for Printed Library Materials, ANSI/NISO Z39.48-1992.

CONTENTS

CONTENTS vii

INTRODUCTION

Critical thinking is a process of reasoning by which one can decide what to believe and what to do. The focus is on reasoning and on the development of good habits of reasoning. The critical thinker continually asks questions: Is that statement true? What reasons are given for me to believe that a statement is true? Are they good reasons? Why or why not? Do the several reasons given support the conclusion that the statement is true? If so, how do they support it? Are there also reasons to believe the statement is false? What are those reasons? Are they good reasons? Why or why not? How do the reasons given support the conclusion that the statement is false? Are the reasons to believe the statement is true better reasons than the reasons to believe the statement is false? Why or why not?

In its most abstract form, critical thinking is similar to logic, which focuses on the evaluation of arguments. Critical thinking is more than that, however. Logic is concerned with the quality of arguments. Logicians, as logicians, don't worry about the content of the arguments they evaluate. They are typically concerned with the structures or *forms* of arguments and the criteria for evaluating arguments of those forms. The content is often secondary; in a symbolic logic course, the content of the argument is irrelevant. The critical thinker must be concerned with the form of the argument, but she must also be concerned with the argument's content. She must ask whether the statements given to support the conclusion reasonably can be taken to be true since the focus of the critical thinker is on the practical application of reasoning.

Regardless of the discipline in which we focus our efforts, we all want good reasons to support the conclusions we reach. We all want to be critical thinkers. The *criteria* we use to determine whether a document is a genuine Declaration of Independence, for example, differ from the *criteria* we use to determine whether investing in General Electric will (probably) yield better returns over the next ten years than investing in General Motors. In determining whether a document is a genuine copy of the Declaration of Independence, one might examine the paper, the ink used, and the handwriting to see whether they are the same as in what is known to be a genuine copy of the Declaration of Independence. In comparing stocks, one might look for consistency in growth of earnings and dividends, a positive price-to-earnings ratio below fifteen, a low price-to-book-value ratio, a fairly stable stock price, and financial strength (financial reserves of over one billion dollars). But the *process* of reasoning—the kind of arguments we use to reach a decision—is similar in the two cases. Critical thinking is concerned with the evaluative processes that are common to virtually any kind of decision we reach.

In the following pages we sketch some of the central critical thinking issues. At some points you'll probably say it sounds like logic, as well it might. The "critical thinking movement" developed, in part, as a rebellion against the highly symbolic systems of modern logic; it attempts to cover much of the logic without using symbols. While the focus in modern symbolic logic is largely theoretical, the focus in critical thinking is on the practical application of what logic teaches. If you want to distill critical thinking to its most basic issues, they can probably be summed up in four questions:

1. What does a sentence (statement, proposition) claim?
2. Is the statement true (or false)?
3. What reasons are there to believe that the statement is true (or false)?
4. How good are the reasons to believe that the statement is true (or false)?

The first question is often answered easily. We won't spend a lot of time on it. The second question can be conclusively answered less often than one might expect. The third and fourth questions focus on argument, which will be our primary concern throughout.

This is a handbook. It is *not* intended to be a critical thinking textbook: there is neither a wealth of examples to illustrate points nor a bank of exercises on which to hone skills regarding the topics covered.[1] Rather, it covers critical thinking issues succinctly and offers an example or two to illustrate each point. If you are concerned with critical thinking skills as they are exemplified in a particular discipline, for example, economics, history, or political science, the account should be sufficient to allow you to find similar examples in your discipline. Some points will be covered rather quickly since they're "obvious." They are there for two reasons: (1) Some points are "obvious" only after they're brought consciously before the mind, and (2) improvement in critical thinking skills usually requires that the relevant points be brought consciously before the mind. At other points the authors are likely to go into more detail than you might want. On those occasions the principal points are made early in the discussion, and the more detailed discussion is headed "A Logical Digression." A Logical Digression often contains the logical underpinnings of the position discussed, and it is often somewhat more technical than the earlier discussion. Since there are various technical terms that might be interesting, perhaps even useful, but that are not essential to understanding the material, the authors also include an occasional discussion of odd words. The Odd Words discussions are numbered individually, but might be placed within a more general discussion. Both Logical Digressions and Odd Word discussions are set off from the rest of the text.

Since this is a handbook, we try to acquaint the readers with all the types of arguments that they might encounter. Some of these types of reasoning are controversial. There is no universal agreement about the right criteria for evaluating all types of arguments. However, it is important for the reader to be aware of the standards that they might encounter. So we have endeavored to include all the types one might observe.

It is the authors' hope that you will find this a useful guide, review, and reference.

NOTE

1. For those interested in exercises, see our Web page at www.rowmanlittlefield .com.

Dilbert on Critical Thinking

①

WORD HAZARDS: STATEMENTS, AMBIGUITY, AND VAGUENESS

Words are hazardous. If we're going to make reasonable decisions, we need to know what statements are true. Typically, to determine whether a statement is true, we must understand the sentence that expresses it. And there we confront those perilous words.

Let us start by defining some terms. As used in this book, a *statement* or *proposition* is what is expressed by a declarative sentence, a purely rhetorical question, or, in some contexts, an exclamation. A statement is either *true* or *false*: This is the defining characteristic of a statement. It's true if it corresponds to the way the world is; otherwise, it is false. Although every statement *is* true or false, we often don't *know* whether a statement is true or false. In many cases we do not have good grounds for *believing* that it's true (even if we *do* believe it is true and even if it *is* true). Whether we believe, or doubt, or have an opinion about the truth or falsehood of a statement is an issue that is independent of *whether* the statement is true or false.[1] Our beliefs don't make statements true or false; facts about the world do. Although many have believed the earth to be flat, it is approximately spherical.

If we want to know what proposition is asserted by a sentence, we usually need to know what the words in the sentence mean. If we do not know what a word means, we look it up in a dictionary. But if we look up a typical noun in a dictionary, we often discover that the word has several meanings. The word is *ambiguous*. If you hear the sentence "A cat crossed the street," what crossed the street? Was it a small animal? A large animal? A piece of earthmoving equipment? A jazz musician? A fish? A sailboat? The context will usually help you judge which meaning is intended. So, for example, an *easy* test is probably not sexually promiscuous.

Poorly constructed sentences can also be ambiguous. When Captain Spaulding says, "Last week I shot an elephant in my pajamas,"[2] it's only after you hear the next sentence, "What he was doing in my pajamas I don't know," that the ambiguity is resolved. Had the first sentence been more complete, "Last week I shot an elephant that was wearing my pajamas," there would have been no ambiguity—and no laughs.

Words such as "many," "several," and "a few" are *vague*. If several cats crossed the street, you don't know how many cats crossed the street. Most of the time, this makes little difference. Sometimes you want a higher degree of *precision*. Six cats crossed the street. And sometimes precision can be overdone. The fellow who said, "Our son was born on June 29, 1983. Our daughter was born on July 1, 1986. We wanted our children born three years apart—but we failed," probably subscribed to an unreasonably high expectation of precision.

Some words can be hazardous because of their emotional connotations: In some cases a word with a favorable emotional connotation can sway one to accept a statement as true. Words such as *peace* and *love* have positive emotional connotations. Who can be opposed to peace and love? But for that very reason it is important to be very certain what the writer or speaker means by the words. The former German Democratic Republic (East Germany) was neither a democracy nor a republic in the commonly assumed senses of those terms, no matter how favorable the emotional connotations of the words "democracy" and "republic" might be. Emotionally charged terms can sway one's judgment. When an argument contains emotionally charged terms, it is often wise to replace the emotionally charged terms with emotionally neutral terms that have the same cognitive meaning. This allows one to determine whether one is swayed by the emotional connotations or the content of the argument. If John is an *embezzler* (positive connotation), he's still a *crook* (negative connotation), that is, a *thief* (more neutral connotation).

1.1.1 A Logical Digression: Propositional Attitudes

Every statement is either true or false, but when one introduces various propositional attitudes such as knowing or believing, additional relations are involved. Consider knowing. If one knows that a proposition is true, the proposition must be true: Where p is a statement or proposition, one of the conditions for using the word "know" is that if one knows that p, p must be true. If one does *not* know that p, it *does not follow* that p is false. Consider the many years when no one knew that the earth is not the center of the universe. *Knowledge* is often defined as justified, true belief. So, if one knows that p, p must be true, p must be believed, and there must be reasons to believe that p is true (the belief that p is true must be justified). If one does not know that p, then *either* p is false, *or* p is not believed, *or* there are not (or are not sufficient) reasons to believe that p is true. One might have many false beliefs. One might also have beliefs that are true but for which one has insufficient evidence to show that one's belief is true.

There are relations among propositional attitudes. For example, one cannot at once believe that a proposition is true and doubt that the same proposition is true. That would be an *inconsistency* in propositional attitude. There is no inconsistency, however, in believing p at one time and doubting p at another. Examples: "Juan used to believe that the Bible is literally true, but now he doubts that some biblical claims can be taken at face value." "Sara now believes that some of her income should be saved, but she used to believe that it all should be spent." Similarly, one cannot consistently know that p and doubt that p since knowledge involves belief. But *here* the time factor plays no role: If Sonja *knew* that p was true some time ago, she cannot consistently doubt that p is true now, so long as p is the same proposition. It would be consistent, however, if several years ago she believed that she knew that p is true but now doubts that p is true.

A word or two should be said about time and truth. Before July 20, 1969, the proposition, "Some human being has walked on the moon" was false; after July 20, 1969, it was true. Sometimes temporal references are implicit, and there are implications regarding propositional attitudes. For example, if in 1999 Sonja *knew* that Bill Clinton was president of the United States, she could *not* now *doubt* that Bill Clinton was president *in 1999*. If she knew in 1999 that Bill Clinton was the current president of the United States, she might doubt that Clinton is *now* the current president, since allusions to "the current president" contain a temporal reference.

NOTES

1. Knowing, believing, doubting, affirming, opining, and so on are known as propositional attitudes. In our first Logical Digression we shall consider the relationships among some of these propositional attitudes.

2. *Animal Crackers* (Paramount Pictures, 1930).

2

COMPLEX PASSAGES: DESCRIPTIONS, EXPLANATIONS, AND ARGUMENTS

Complex passages are composed of statements. The statements are linked together in various ways and answer various questions.

Descriptions answer the questions Who? What? When? Where? and sometimes How? Descriptions provide information. When it answers the question How? it tells how something is, *not* how it came to be. Most of the information we read or hear is descriptive. It is *accurate* to the extent that the propositions it contains are true. Example: "Franklin Delano Roosevelt was the thirty-second president of the United States. He served as president from 1933 to 1945. He was the only president who was elected to six consecutive terms." Some of the information is accurate—the first two statements are true—and some is inaccurate: The last statement is false. Descriptions can also be more or less *complete*. Any description of Roosevelt's presidency is woefully incomplete if it ignores his actions during the Depression of the 1930s and World War II. Example: "The White House is a building in Washington, D.C." is incomplete insofar as it leaves out its best-known characteristic: The White House is the residence of the president of the United States.

Explanations answer the question Why? and sometimes How? When an explanation answers the question How? it explains how to do something or how something came to be. Examples: (1) There is a pot of boiling water on my stove. You want to know why. I explain: "I'm planning to boil spaghetti for supper." (2) There is a pot of boiling water on my stove. You want to know why the water is boiling. The explanation might be: "All water heated to 212°F boils. The water on the stove is water heated to 212°F. So, the water on the stove is boiling." An alternative explanation might be: "Heat passes through the pan, causing the molecules of water to move more rapidly. This results in visible movements in the water which we call 'boiling.'" Notice that the phenomenon to be explained is known prior to the principles that provide the explanation. In the discussion of inductive arguments, we consider criteria for evaluating explanations.

2.1.1 Odd Words

People who spend a lot of time talking about explanations call the description of the phenomenon to be explained the *explanandum*. They call the statements that do the explaining the *explanans*.

An *argument* is a discourse in which one or more statements, the *premises*, are taken as reasons to believe that another statement, the *conclusion*, is true. As used in this book, an argument *does not* presuppose a disagreement, although it is common for arguments to support one or another side of an *issue*. An issue is some subject about which there is disagreement. The premises are known or assumed to be true prior to knowing that the conclusion is true. In terms of appearance, an argument is often indistinguishable from an explanation. One can determine whether a discourse is an argument or an explanation on the basis of the context in which it is given: The context will generally allow one to determine what is *assumed*.

Arguments are generally divided into two classes: *deductive* arguments and *inductive* arguments. The distinction is both somewhat misleading and somewhat arbitrary. It would be better put as follows: *Every argument is a valid deductive argument or it is an inductive argument.* *Validity* concerns the structure or *form* of an argument. For example, the following two arguments have the same form:

If John went to the store, then Martha made mincemeat.
John went to the store.
Therefore, Martha made mincemeat.

If the stock market averages continue to rise and the unemployment rate declines, then we will have a booming economy.

The stock market averages continue to rise and the unemployment rate declines.
Therefore, we will have a booming economy.

Where p and q are variables that can be replaced by statements, the *form* of the argument can be represented as follows:

If p, then q.
p
Therefore, q.

Validity is a property of an argument form. If an argument form is *valid*, then it is impossible for all its premises to be true and its conclusion false. Validity is independent of the actual content of an argument. (Later chapters concern valid forms and how to show that the forms are valid.) If an argument form is valid and its premises are true, the argument is said to be *sound*. It is impossible for the conclusion of a sound argument to be false.

Insofar as an inductive argument is anything short of a valid deductive argument, it is *always* possible for the premises to be true and the conclusion false. *Most* invalid deductive arguments (inductive arguments) provide little evidence for the truth of their conclusions. Several kinds of common inductive arguments—"arguments to a generalization, analogies, arguments to the best explanation"—provide limited evidence for the truth of their conclusions. No inductive arguments are valid or sound, but some inductive arguments are *stronger* than others. As we shall see, there are various criteria that can be used to judge the strength of different kinds of inductive arguments.

The distinction might be put this way: A *sound* deductive argument—a valid deductive argument with true premises—provides *conclusive* evidence for the truth of its conclusion, while a *cogent* inductive argument—a strong inductive argument with true premises—only shows that it is probable its conclusion is true.

While the distinction between a valid deductive argument and an inductive argument is exclusive and exhaustive—every argument is either a valid deductive argument or an inductive argument, and no argument is both—the distinction is somewhat arbitrary insofar as any inductive argument can be reformulated as a valid deductive argument. Consider the following analogy (an inductive argument):

Luis and Lucinda are alike insofar as they are both English majors and they have a particular interest in modern poetry.

Luis liked Professor Smith's course on Yeats.
Therefore, (it is likely that) Lucinda will like Professor Smith's course on Yeats.

It's possible that both the premises are true and the conclusion is false. But it can be reformulated as a valid deductive argument:

If Luis and Lucinda are alike insofar as they are both English majors and they have a particular interest in modern poetry and Luis liked Professor Smith's course on Yeats, then Lucinda will like Professor Smith's course on Yeats.
Luis and Lucinda are alike insofar as they are both English majors and they have a particular interest in modern poetry and Luis liked Professor Smith's course on Yeats.
Therefore, Lucinda will like Professor Smith's course on Yeats.

The analogy provides *some* evidence that the conclusion is true. On the other hand, since the deductive argument is valid, *if* the premises are true, then the conclusion must be true as well. Does one provide better evidence for the truth of the conclusion than the other?

No. Validity, as such, does not guarantee that the conclusion is true. It only guarantees that the conclusion is true if the premises are also true. In reformulating the analogy as a valid deductive argument, there is a shift in focus. While in both cases there is reason to believe that the conclusion is true only if the premises are true, in the case of the deductive argument there is reason to question the truth of the conditional (*if . . ., then . . .*) premise. That is, there is reason to believe it is quite possible that even though Luis and Lucinda are alike in the ways specified and Luis liked Professor Smith's class, Lucinda might not: Lucinda and Professor Smith might have a personality conflict, for example. In the inductive argument, the premises provide *some reason to believe* that the conclusion is true. In the valid deductive argument they do as well, but the *confidence* you can ascribe to the truth of the conclusion is no greater than the confidence you can ascribe to its weakest premise. Since there is only some reason to believe that the conditional premise is true, there is only some reason to believe that the conclusion is true.

2.1.2 A Logical Digression: How Not to Distinguish Induction from Deduction, or Why the Valid/Inductive Distinction Is Better

Every valid deductive argument provides conclusive evidence for the truth of its conclusion *if* its premises are true. The *validity* of an argument is a property of its form (structure). No invalid deductive argument provides conclusive evidence for the truth of its conclusion *even if* its premises are true. The *invalidity* of an argument is a property of its form. Because validity is a property of an argument's form, every argument is valid or it is not; the distinction between valid and invalid arguments is exclusive and exhaustive. No inductive argument is a valid deductive argument; that is, all inductive arguments are formally invalid; that is, it is always possible for all the premises of an inductive argument to be true and its conclusion to be false. So, our questions are: If every argument form is either valid or invalid and all inductive arguments are invalid, is anything gained by talking of "deductive arguments" as such? Isn't it at least as reasonable to drop the term "deductive argument" and contend that the distinction is between valid arguments and inductive arguments? We argue that the answer to the first question is negative and the answer to the second question is positive by showing that several common ways in which the deductive/inductive distinction is drawn are misguided or unhelpful.

Some people distinguish induction from deduction in the following way: In an inductive argument one proceeds from particular premises (or singular premises, that is, premises concerning individuals) to a general conclusion. In a deductive argument, one proceeds from general premises to a particular conclusion. *That doesn't work.* Everyone would grant that the following two arguments are valid deductive arguments:

All mortals are things that eventually die.
All humans are mortals.
Therefore, all humans are things that eventually die.

If Alejandro went to the game, then Solvig went to the dance.
Alejandro went to the game.
Therefore, Solvig went to the dance.

In the first argument, all the component statements are general. In the second, all the component statements are singular. On the other hand, analogies are inductive arguments in which one proceeds directly from one particular (or singular) case to another (there is no generalization):

Lucinda and Megan are alike insofar as they both like rap music and heavy metal music.
Lucinda also likes classic rock and roll.
So, it is likely that Megan also likes classic rock and roll.[1]

Thus, there are arguments that everyone would grant are deductive but do not proceed from general propositions to particular or singular propositions. Similarly, there are inductive arguments that do not proceed from particular or singular propositions to general propositions. Hence, the proposed deductive/inductive distinction fails.

Second, some people distinguish induction from deduction by claiming that while deductive arguments yield conclusions that are *certain* (certainly true), inductive arguments yield conclusions that are only *probable* (probably true). This is either false or misleading. *Sound* deductive arguments— valid deductive arguments with true premises—establish conclusively that their conclusions are true. If one has a sound argument and one *knows* that the premises are true, then one can be certain of the conclusion—one can know that the conclusion is true. Unfortunately, one seldom is certain that the premises are true. Hence, even if an argument is *in fact* sound, it will not yield certainty unless one knows that the premises are true. If one does *not know* that the premises of valid argument are true, one can ascribe no greater certainty to the conclusion than one ascribes to the weakest premise, that is, the premise to which one ascribes the least certainty. Hence, the conclusion of many sound deductive arguments can be asserted with only a certain degree of probability. Hence, attempts to distinguish deduction from induction on the grounds of certainty versus probability fail.[2]

Third, one might suggest that the distinction between induction and deduction is based on the arguer's intentions. In the case of a deductive argument, it would be said that the arguer *intends* it to provide conclusive evidence for the conclusion if its premises are true, while in the case of an inductive argument the arguer *intends* that it provide only a certain degree of evidence if its premises are true. This will not work either. Validity is an objective property of an argument form. Procedures are discussed in subsequent chapters by which one can conclusively—indeed, mechanically— determine whether an argument form is valid. No one trained in logic can seriously intend that certain invalid "deductive" forms provide certainty for their conclusions since he or she would have no reason to believe that certain notoriously invalid forms with true premises provide conclusive evidence for their conclusions. On the other hand, someone without training in logic might *intend* that an inductive argument provides conclusive evidence for its conclusion. If an inductive/deductive distinction were based on the arguer's intentions, there would be no hard-and-fast distinction.

Fourth, nor is it plausible to contend that a distinction should be drawn between invalid deductive forms and inductive forms insofar as *some* inductive forms are so implausible that no one would seriously contend that the premises provide evidence for their conclusions. "Inductive" would, then, be an honorific term for those invalid forms that are often or generally taken to provide limited evidence for their conclusions. While granting that some invalid forms lack plausibility, historically, different types of inductive argument forms have gone in and out of style. Inference to the best explanation is popular today. It was not popular in the 1920s and 1930s. One might argue that what the nineteenth-century philosopher C. S. Peirce called "abduction" is similar in many ways to what is now called "inference to the best explanation." Indeed, one might argue that what the ancient geometer Pappus and some late medieval and early modern philosophers called "analysis" is now called "inference to the best explanation." But historical accident is hardly a good ground for distinguishing "inductive" forms from invalid but out-of-favor argument forms. So, we reject this basis for a deductive/inductive distinction as well.

Since validity pertains to all argument forms, since there are objective means to determine whether an argument form is valid, and since the distinction between valid forms and invalid (inductive) forms is exclusive and exhaustive, we believe the proper distinction is between valid arguments and inductive arguments.[3]

NOTES

1. Some people contend that there is an implicit generalization involved in an analogy. So, they claim that from "Lucinda and Megan are alike insofar as they both like rap music and heavy metal music" one concludes that "Lucinda and Megan like all kinds of music," and from this and the second premise the conclusion that Megan likes classical rock and roll follows with validity. But the generalization is implausible. Assume that Lucinda and Megan are typical American teenagers. Assume that typical American teenagers might like both rap and heavy metal music. From this, it hardly follows that they like *all* kinds of music; relatively few typical American teenagers like Bach toccatas or atonal music. So, while the analogy has some plausibility when taken to go from singular statements to another singular statement, it is becomes implausible when it is taken to include an implicit generalization. Were one to claim that our generalization is too broad, it is extremely difficult to determine the limits of the generalization. It cannot be limited to "popular music" since that includes country and western music, which many teenagers find repugnant. Indeed, any attempt to limit the generalization would appear to be *ad hoc*. Hence, it is unreasonable to claim that there is an implicit generalization operative in an analogy. For a more complete discussion of analogies, see chapter 9.

2. Some might object that this discussion concerns only *epistemic* certainty, while the proper concern is with *logical* certainty. But an argument is logically

certain if and only if it is valid; that is, it is impossible for all the premises to be true and the conclusion false. So, if the concern is with *logical* certainty, we grant the point while maintaining that this provides even better reason to drop considerations of certainty for considerations of validity. Invalid arguments, of course, cannot claim logical certainty.

3. Some offer a trifold distinction between deductive, inductive, and *abductive* arguments. On such proposals, inductive is often taken to employ quantitative and abductive qualitative standards. Thus, generalizations and particularizations (chapter 8) are usually said to be inductive, and explanatory inferences (chapter 10) are usually said to be abductive. However, this is problematic for two reasons. First, it is unclear where to put analogical arguments (chapter 9). Second, there are explanatory inferences that purport to use quantitative standards, such as those that employ Bayes's theorem. Thus, the trifold distinction is far from being clear and neat. It is better to distinguish arguments in terms of valid/inductive and then to distinguish among inductive arguments in terms of their degree of strength, which comes in many varieties.

3

FINDING ARGUMENTS

Finding arguments is like finding money: Just as it's more likely to find loose change in a parking lot than in a hay field, you're more likely to find arguments on the opinion page of a newspaper than on the front page. Nonetheless, just as getting into the right neighborhood won't guarantee you'll find the house for which you are looking, just knowing where to look won't guarantee you'll find arguments. There are additional techniques that help you find arguments.

There are various words that are commonly called *premise* and *conclusion indicators*. Here is a partial list of premise indicators:

since	for	given (that)
due to	inasmuch as	from
†follows from	†may be deduced	†as shown by
because	as	assuming (that)
in view of the fact that	insofar as	†as indicated by
†may be derived from	†may be inferred from	†the reason is that

In the expressions marked with a dagger (†) the conclusion usually precedes the premise indicator. Here is a partial list of conclusion indicators:

therefore	°is evidence that	so
thus	hence	°implies that

accordingly	°which means that	°which allows us to in-
I conclude that	as a result	fer that
°means that	for this reason	°which points to the
in consequence	°which entails that	conclusion that
ergo	for these reasons	°is a reason to believe
°which shows that	it follows that	that
consequently	°which implies that	°is a reason to hold
proves that	we may infer	that

In the expressions marked with an asterisk (°), one or more premises usually precede the conclusion indicator.

Some people place great stock in premise and conclusion indicators, but they must be used with considerable caution. (1) Not all premises and conclusions are marked with indicator words. (2) *As* indicator words, they intrinsically appeal to claims of truth: "Since (it is true that) *p*, we may conclude (it is true that) *q*." (3) Many of the same words are often used in explanations. There the premise indicators point to the explaining factors (the *explanans*), and the conclusion indicators point to the description of the phenomenon to be explained (the *explanandum*). (4) Some of the words are used in contexts that have nothing to do with arguments: *Since* is used to show a passage of time, for example. (5) Sometimes elements of the argument are unstated: One or more of the premises or the conclusion is unstated. These are known as *enthymemes* or *enthymematic arguments*. Overall, if one can locate the conclusion of the argument, one is probably better served by asking, "What reasons are given (or assumed) that show the conclusion is true?" When the argument is enthymematic, context often helps one figure out what is not stated.[1]

If one is going to carefully examine an argument, it is useful to carefully *reconstruct* it by explicitly laying out the premises and conclusion or conclusions:

Premise 1:
Premise 2:
. . .
Premise *n*:
Conclusion:

There are several reasons for this. (1) It allows one to clearly see how the argument goes. One of the nasty things about ordinary prose is that it often contains extraneous information that one leaves out in the reconstruction. (2) One can see whether the way the argument was presented is the tightest way it can be presented. The *principle of charity* requires that when reconstructing an argument, one must make the argument as strong as the original verbiage permits. This means that if it can be reconstructed as a valid deductive argument with true premises, it should be so stated. If treating it as a valid deductive argument would require assuming it has a false premise—for example, a false universal premise—it is more charitable to treat it as an inductive argument. For example, if one had to choose between the following two reconstructions,

A   All swans are white.
     All the birds on this lake are swans.
     Therefore, all the birds on this lake are white.
and

B   Most swans are white.
     All the birds on this lake are swans.
     Therefore, all the birds on this lake are (probably) white.

one should choose the second since some Australian swans are black (the first premise of argument A is false). Or one might build a context into the argument:

C   All North American swans are white.
     All the birds on this lake are North American swans.
     Therefore, all the birds on this lake are white.

Of the three, argument C is best (assuming the second premise is true) since it provides the strongest support for the conclusion: It is a *sound* argument.

Of course, there are limits to charity. One should not be more charitable than the original verbiage allows. For example, if you confronted the enthymematic argument

No two-year-olds are readers, so no two-year-olds are cooks.

the missing premise *has* to be "All cooks are readers" since that is the *only* premise that would yield a valid argument. That premise, of course, is false. In some cases one might need to provide several reconstructions, indicating the strengths and weaknesses of each.

NOTE

1. As we'll see below, in the case of valid deductive enthymematic arguments, there are ways to figure out what the missing premise or conclusion *must* be.

4

GROUNDING STATEMENTS IN FACT: OBSERVATION, TESTIMONY, AND OTHER ARGUMENTS BASED ON CRITERIA

We need to know whether the statements that provide the premises for arguments are true or, at least, are probably true. We need to *ground* our statements in fact.

In many cases, we ground our statements on the basis of observation or testimony. There are criteria for evaluating the probable truth of observation statements and testimony. These criteria provide guidelines for making a decision. If a statement rates well on the relevant set of criteria, you have good grounds for *accepting it as true*. As we shall see, however, a "thumbs up" on each of the criteria *does not guarantee* that the statement is true. The criteria provide only inductive evidence.

4.1 CRITERIA FOR EVALUATING OBSERVATION STATEMENTS

O1. The observer has the faculties sufficient to make the observation.
O2. The observer was in conditions adequate (relative to their faculties of observation) to make the observation.
O3. Any technology used by the observer was itself sufficient and in conditions adequate to make the observation.
O4. The observer has the background knowledge necessary to accurately recognize and report what is being observed.

O5. The observer has the open-mindedness necessary to report what is being observed without bias.

O6. There is no other reason to think that what is being observed did not occur or that it was not observed (even if it did occur).

4.2 CRITERIA FOR EVALUATING TESTIMONY

T1. The person offering the testimony has the rational faculties sufficient to conclude reasonably that the claim is true.

T2. The person offering the testimony is generally reliable.

T3. The person offering the testimony has sufficient training and/or experience to draw the conclusion.

T4. The person does not have motivation to misinterpret (accidentally or intentionally) the facts they are considering.

T5. The testimony is consistent with what other reliable sources would claim.

T6. There is no other reason to believe that the claim being made is false or that the person testifying should not be trusted.

These criteria require a few comments.

First, it is always possible that a particular case can rate high on all the criteria and still be worthy of rejection. Assume that Professor Jones is generally reliable, a well-trained and respected expert in her field, stands to lose more in reputation by being wrong than she would gain in any way if she were right, is presenting testimony that is consistent with the views of other experts in her field, and is (apparently) free from bias. If Professor Jones says, "The English philosopher John Locke (1632–1704) always used the word 'idea' to refer to mental images," the claim could still be false. Before Copernicus, virtually all the experts agreed that the earth is center of the universe. Similarly, one could rate low regarding all the observation criteria and still make a true statement. The criteria tend to show that there are—or are not—good grounds for believing that an observation statement or a piece of testimony is true; *whether* the statement is true is a distinct issue.

Second, some of the criteria generally carry more weight than the others. For example, if Jamal claimed he saw a bank robbery at 129 Main Street at noon but at the time Jamal was twenty blocks away, there is reason to question his claim. The *burden of proof* falls on Jamal to explain how that was possible: "I saw it on a surveillance camera," he explains. (Most of us have *seen* the World Trade Center Towers fall—and we've probably seen them fall several times—on television, even though few of us were in New York

City on September 11, 2001.) Inconsistency between a statement and what is "known" from other sources shows that both statements cannot be true.

Typically, criteria such as those above need to be discussed individually, and some assessment needs to be made of their relative weight. Often this will involve a certain amount of conversation and argument regarding the relative weight that should be assigned to a given criterion. Biased observation by a witness in a murder case might be a very good ground for questioning his testimony. It is not clear that you can say the same regarding a scientist whose observations are "biased" by her hypothesis.

The criteria above are simply examples of the use of criteria as the basis for an inductive argument. Virtually every field has criteria that are used as guidelines for reaching decisions. There are well-established criteria to guide your investment strategies, although the relative weight assigned to any one criterion in a given situation is the basis for an inductive argument. There are criteria to determine the probable authenticity of a historical document or a work of art, although, again, the relative weight of a given criterion in a particular situation is open to inductive argument.

5

DEDUCTION: CATEGORICAL SYLLOGISMS

A valid deductive argument with true premises—a *sound* argument— provides conclusive evidence for the truth of its conclusion. Discussions of deduction focus on the *form* or the structure of an argument; issues concerning the truth of the premises of any given argument, while essential to careful reasoning, are independent of considerations of deductive validity.

Categorical syllogisms concern relations of inclusion and exclusion among classes (categories) of things. The study of categorical syllogisms dates back to Aristotle (384–322 B.C.E.). Categorical syllogisms are composed of categorical propositions, of which there are four general forms. Where *S* is the subject term and *P* is the predicate term, there are four distinct kinds of categorical propositions:

Type of Proposition	Form	Example
Universal Affirmative	All *S* are *P*.	All beagles are dogs.
Universal Negative	No *S* are *P*.	No cats are dogs.
Particular Affirmative	Some *S* are *P*.	Some dogs are beagles.
Particular Negative	Some *S* are not *P*.	Some dogs are not beagles.

In ordinary English, of course, there are many ways to say *all*, *no*, *some . . . are . . .* , and *some . . . are not. . . .* The word *some* is understood to mean "at least one."

We represented the form by letters rather than by words. Why? When we
are concerned only with the form or structure of a statement or argument,
the content makes no difference. A universal affirmative proposition has the
form "All *S* are *P*" whether the proposition is "All beagles are dogs" or
"Everyone who attended the president's inaugural ball was a person who
contributed generously to the president's campaign either monetarily or
through hard labor." By replacing the terms with variables, we can more
easily "see" the form of the statement. In an argument, stating the argument in terms of variables allows one to see clearly how the parts of the argument fit together. Since the validity of an argument and the logical equivalence of statement forms concern *only* forms, symbols provide a
convenient and perspicuous shorthand.

5.1 CONVERSION, OBVERSION, CONTRAPOSITION

There are logically equivalent forms of each of the categorical propositions.
Two statements are *logically equivalent* if and only if they are true under exactly the same circumstances.

The *converse* of a categorical proposition is formed by switching the positions of the subject and predicate terms. In the case of universal negative
propositions and particular affirmative propositions, the converse of the
proposition is logically equivalent to the given proposition. In the case of
universal affirmative propositions and particular negative propositions, the
converse of the proposition is *not* logically equivalent to the given proposition.

Given Proposition	Converse
All *S* are *P*.	*not logically equivalent*
No *S* are *P*.	No *P* are *S*.
Some *S* are *P*.	Some *P* are *S*.
Some *S* are not *P*.	*not logically equivalent*

Examples: "All beagles are dogs" is true, but its converse, "All dogs are beagles," is false. "No cats are dogs" is true, as is its converse, "No dogs are
cats." "Some dogs are beagles" is true, as is its converse, "Some beagles are
dogs." (Remember: the meaning of "Some *S* are *P*" is "There is at least one
thing that is both *S* and *P*.") "Some dogs are not beagles" is true, but its converse, "Some beagles are not dogs," is false. This is *not* to say that there are
no cases in which both a universal affirmative proposition and its converse

are true; it is only that the truth or falsehood of a universal affirmative proposition does not guarantee that its converse also will be true. In the case of a universal affirmative proposition that reflects a definition, its converse is true if the given universal is true. For example, the statement, "All bachelors are unmarried men," and its converse, "All unmarried men are bachelors," are both true.

The *obverse* of a categorical proposition is always logically equivalent to the given categorical proposition. The obverse is formed by changing the quality of the proposition from affirmative to negative or negative to affirmative and replacing the predicate with its complement. The complement of a class of objects is that class of objects that contains all objects that are *not* in the class. For example, the complement of the class of objects that are cats contains everything that is *not* a cat. The complement of the term *cats* is *non-cats*.[1]

Given Proposition	Obverse
All S are P.	No S are non-P.
No S are P.	All S are non-P.
Some S are P.	Some S are not non-P.
Some S are not P.	Some S are non-P.

The *contrapositive* of a categorical proposition is formed by converting the proposition and replacing each term with its complement. In the case of universal affirmative and particular negative propositions, the contrapositive of the proposition is logically equivalent to the given proposition. In the case of universal negative propositions and particular affirmative propositions, the contrapositive of the proposition is *not* logically equivalent to the given proposition.

Given Proposition	Contrapositive
All S are P.	All non-P are non-S.
Some S are P.	not logically equivalent
Some S are P.	not logically equivalent
Some S are not P.	Some non-P are not non-S.

Examples: "All beagles are dogs" is true, as is its contrapositive, "All non-dogs are non-beagles." "No cats are dogs" is true, but its contrapositive, "No non-dogs are non-cats," is false: an elephant is both a non-cat and a non-dog. "Some dogs are beagles" and its contrapositive, "Some non-beagles are non-dogs," are both true, but they pick out different objects. Fido might be both a dog and a beagle, but the U.S.S. *Constitution* is both a non-dog and a non-beagle. "Some dogs are not beagles" is true under the same conditions as "Some non-beagles are not non-dogs."

5.2 CATEGORICAL SYLLOGISMS

A syllogism is a deductive argument consisting of two premises and a conclusion. A categorical syllogism is a syllogism in which the premises and the conclusion are categorical propositions and that contains *exactly* three terms which are assigned the same meaning throughout.[2] Examples of categorical syllogisms:

All cows are mammals.	No cats are dogs.
All Jerseys are cows.	All tabbies are cats.
Therefore, all Jerseys are mammals.	Therefore, no tabbies are dogs.

The terms in a categorical syllogism each have a name. The predicate term of the conclusion is called the *major term*. The major term in the first syllogism above is "mammals"; the major term in the second syllogism is "dogs." The subject term of the conclusion is the *minor term*. The minor term in the first syllogism is "Jerseys"; the minor term in the second syllogism is "tabbies." The term that is in both premises but not in the conclusion is the *middle term*. The middle term of the first syllogism is "cows"; the middle term of the second syllogism is "cats." The *major premise* contains the major term; the *minor premise* contains the minor term. By a longstanding tradition, a syllogism is said to be in *standard form* when it is set up with the major premise on the first line, the minor premise on the second line, and the conclusion on the third line.[3] Both syllogisms above are in standard form.

The primary concern with syllogisms is validity. A categorical syllogism is valid if it is impossible for all of its premises to be true and its conclusion to be false. This is a function of the *form* or structure of the syllogism. Let P stand for the major term, S for the minor term, and M for the middle term. You can represent the form of the syllogism with these variables. The forms of the syllogisms above can be represented as follows:

All M are P.	No M are P.
All S are M.	All S are M.
Therefore, all S are P.	Therefore, no S are P.

Since validity is concerned only with the forms of arguments, we shall focus on schematic representations of forms, such as those above.

There are six rules that one can use to judge the validity of categorical syllogisms. To understand these rules, we need to introduce the notion of *distribution*. *A term is distributed if it refers to an entire class.* In a universal affirmative, the subject term is distributed but the predicate term is undistributed: The proposition "All beagles are dogs" says that the entire class of beagles is contained in the class of dogs; it says nothing about the entire class of dogs. In a universal negative, both terms are distributed: The proposition "No dogs are cats" says the entire class of dogs is excluded from the entire class of cats. In a particular affirmative, neither term is distributed: The proposition "Some dogs are beagles" says nothing about the either entire class of dogs or the entire class of beagles. In a particular negative, the predicate term is distributed but the subject term is not distributed: The proposition "Some dogs are not beagles" says at least one dog is excluded from the entire class of beagles. Where D means distributed and U means undistributed, distribution is summarized in the following chart:

All S^D are P^U.
No S^D are P^D.
Some S^U are P^U.
Some S^U are not P^D.

Once we have the notion of distribution, we can state rules for evaluating syllogisms:

1. A syllogism must have exactly three terms that have the same meaning throughout the syllogism.
2. The middle term of a syllogism must be distributed exactly once.
3. The major term must be distributed twice (both in the conclusion and the major premise) or not at all.
4. The minor term must be distributed twice (both in the conclusion and the minor premise) or not at all.
5. The number of negative premises must equal the number of negative conclusions.
6. The number of particular premises must equal the number of particular conclusions.

Given these rules, we can evaluate the validity of *any* categorical syllogism.

Consider a syllogistic form:

All M^D are P^U.
All S^D are M^U.
So, all S^D are P^U.

The distributions of terms are marked to make the application of the rules easier. Since we have a schematic representation of an argument form, we need not worry about the first rule. The middle term is distributed exactly once. The major term is undistributed twice. The minor term is distributed twice. There are neither negative premises nor conclusions. There are neither particular premises nor conclusions. The argument form is valid.

If we have a syllogism—if the variables are replaced with words—we have to pay attention to the first rule. For example, the following syllogism superficially resembles the form above:

All dukes are European aristocrats.
All James Madison University athletes are Dukes.
So, all James Madison University athletes are European aristocrats.

Here we have more than three terms: One use of "dukes" concerns princes of independent duchies, while the other ("Dukes") is a team name. The *argument* breaks the first rule. It is not a categorical syllogism.

Let's look at a few more argument forms. Consider this one:

No P^D are M^D.
Some S^U are M^U.
So, some S^U are not P^D.

Again, since it's the schematic representation of an argument form, we need not worry about rule 1. The middle term is distributed in the major premise but not in the minor premise. The major term is distributed in both the conclusion and the major premise. The minor term is undistributed in both the conclusion and the minor premise. There is one negative premise, and the conclusion is also negative. There is one particular premise, and the conclusion is also particular. The argument form is valid.

Of course, it does not always work out that way:

Some M^U are P^U.
Some M^U are S^U.
No S^D are P^D.

Since it's the schematic representation of an argument form, we need not worry about the first rule. The middle term is undistributed in both premises, so it violates rule 2. The major term is distributed in the conclusion but not in the major premise, so it violates rule 3. The minor term is distributed in the conclusion but not in the minor premise, so it violates rule 4. There are two affirmative premises and a negative conclusion, so it violates rule 5. There are two particular premises and a universal conclusion, so it violates rule 6. Since a syllogistic form is invalid if it violates even one rule, this form is invalid.[4]

There are exactly 256 syllogistic forms: There are sixty-four combinations of the four kinds of propositions arranged as major premise, minor premise, and conclusion, and for each of those, there are four pairs of positions in which the middle term can be found. Of those 256 forms, exactly fifteen are valid.[5] Where the symbol ∴ indicates the conclusion, the fifteen forms are as follows:

All M are P.
All S are M.
∴ All S are P.

All P are M.
No M are S.
∴ No S are P.

All P are M.
No S are M.
∴ No S are P.

All M are P.
Some S are M.
∴ Some S are P.

All M are P.
Some M are S.
∴ Some S are P.

All P are M.
Some S are not M.
∴ Some S are not P.

No M are P.
All S are M.
∴ No S are P.

No P are M.
All S are M.
∴ No S are P.

No M are P.
Some S are M.
∴ Some S are not P.

No P are M.
Some S are M.
∴ Some S are not P.

No M are P.
Some M are S.
∴ Some S are not P.

No P are M.
Some M are S.
∴ Some S are not P.

Some M are P.
All M are S.
∴ Some S are P.

Some P are M.
All M are S.
∴ Some S are P.

Some M are not P.
All M are S.
∴ Some S are not P.

5.2.1 A Logical Digression: Venn Diagrams

The rules provide a perfectly adequate way to evaluate syllogisms. Some people, however, find distribution less than intuitive. Others claim to be "visual learners" and find the entire rule approach counterintuitive. For those people there are Venn diagrams.

Sometime over a century ago, the English mathematician and logician, John Venn (1834–1923) developed a means of evaluating categorical syllogisms by showing relations among areas of circles. Categorical propositions are represented by two-circle diagrams. A bar over an *S* or a *P* indicates that area does *not* contain members of that class. We also illustrate this with the examples regarding beagles, dogs, and cats with which we opened the chapter.

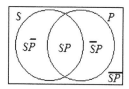
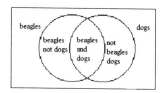

Diagrams for universal propositions show that one area is *empty* by shading the area. So the following diagrams represent universal affirmative and universal negative propositions:

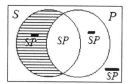
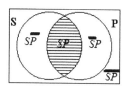

All *S* are *P*.   No *S* are *P*.

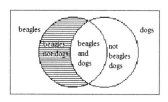
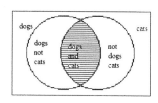

All beagles are dogs.   No dogs are cats.

Notice that we shade the area that is empty. One might think of shaded areas as black holes or some other notion of emptiness. So, if "All beagles are dogs" is true, then there are no beagles that are not dogs. So the area that represents beagles but not dogs is shaded. If "No dogs are cats" is true, then the area that represents dogs that are cats is empty and therefore shaded.[6]

Diagrams for particular propositions show that an area of the diagram is populated—remember, "some" means "at least one"—by placing an X in an area of the diagram. So, the following diagrams represent a particular affirmative and a particular negative:

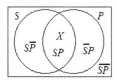

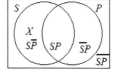

Some S are P.   Some S are not P.

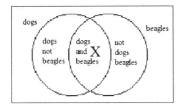

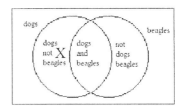

Some dogs are beagles.   Some dogs are not beagles.

When diagramming a categorical syllogism, one uses a three-circle diagram, with one circle representing each of the three classes in a categorical syllogism. The general arrangement is as follows:

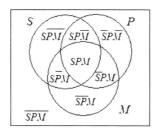

If one treats *S* as *beagles*, *M* as *dogs*, and *P* as *mammals*, and one represents *not* by the tilde (~), the diagram would look like this:

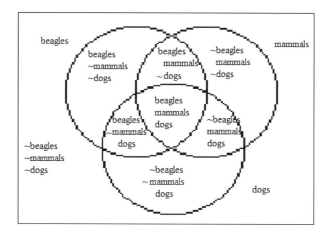

One then diagrams the premises to see whether one also has diagrammed the conclusion. For example, for the following syllogistic form:

All *M* are *P*   All dogs are mammals.
All *S* are *M*.   All beagles are dogs.
∴ All *S* are *P*.   ∴ All beagles are mammals.

the diagram looks like this:

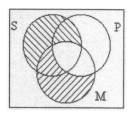   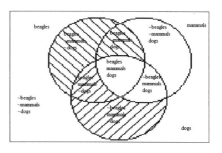

Notice that in diagramming the major premise, one shades all of *M* outside of *P* (dogs that are not mammals). In diagramming the minor premise, one shades all of *S* outside of *M* (beagles that are not mammals). The resulting diagram shows that the only area in *S* that could have members is also in *P* (beagles that are dogs).

The diagram for an argument of the form:

All *M* are *P*.
Some *M* are *S*.
∴ Some *S* are *P*.

looks like this:

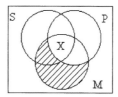

Notice that the *X* is in an area in which *S* and *P* overlap. The argument form is valid.

If the syllogistic form is invalid, diagramming the premises *does not* result in diagramming the conclusion. Consider the syllogistic form:

No *M* are *P*.
No *S* are *M*.
∴ Some *S* are *P*.

The diagram looks like this:

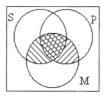

There is no *X* in an area where *S* and *P* overlap. Therefore, the diagram shows that the syllogistic form is invalid.

Consider the syllogistic form:

Some *M* are not *P*.
Some *S* are *M*.
∴ Some *S* are not *P*.

When there is a universal premise, one diagrams it *before* one diagrams a particular premise, since *sometimes* it shows that one of the areas in which the X for the particular premise might be placed is empty. This forces the X into a nonempty region. When there are two particular premises, nothing forces the X into a determinate area. So, the X goes "on the line"; that is, it goes on the line of the circle *not* mentioned in the premise; it goes on the line that divides the relevant two-circle diagram into two parts. So the diagram for the syllogistic form above looks like this:

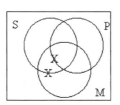

Invalid

The diagrams for the fifteen valid syllogistic forms are as follows:

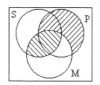

All *M* are *P*.
All *S* are *M*.
∴ All *S* are *P*.

All *P* are *M*.
No *M* are *S*.
∴ No *S* are *P*.

All *P* are *M*.
No *S* are *M*.
∴ No *S* are *P*.

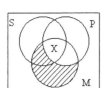

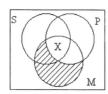

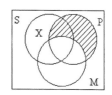

All *M* are *P*.
Some *S* are *M*.
∴ Some *S* are *P*.

All *M* are *P*.
Some *M* are *S*.
∴ Some *S* are *P*.

All *P* are *M*.
Some *S* are not *M*.
∴ Some *S* are not *P*.

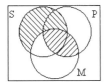

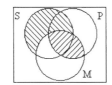

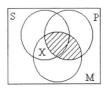

No *M* are *P*.
All *S* are *M*.
∴ No *S* are *P*.

No *P* are *M*.
All *S* are *M*.
∴ No *S* are *P*.

No *M* are *P*.
Some *S* are *M*.
∴ Some *S* are not *P*.

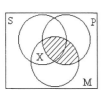

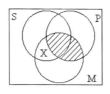

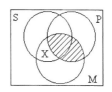

No *P* are *M*.
Some *S* are *M*.
∴ Some *S* are not *P*.

No *M* are *P*.
Some *M* are *S*.
∴ Some *S* are not *P*.

No *P* are *M*.
Some *M* are *S*.
∴ Some *S* are not *P*.

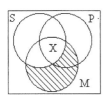

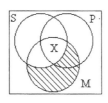

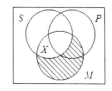

Some *M* are *P*.
All *M* are *S*.
∴ Some *S* are *P*.

Some *P* are *M*.
All *M* are *S*.
∴ Some *S* are *P*.

Some *M* are not *P*.
All *M* are *S*.
∴ Some *S* are not *P*.

5.2.2 A Logical Digression: Conditional Validity

There are two interpretations of categorical logic. The interpretation on which the rules and Venn diagrams rest is the Boolean interpretation, which is named for the nineteenth-century British mathematician and logician George Boole (1815–1864).[7] According to this interpretation, the truth of a universal categorical proposition *does not* require that its subject term pick out an existent thing. This means the proposition "All unicorns are one-horned horses" is true on the Boolean interpretation. It in effect says,

"For anything, if it is a unicorn, then it is a one-horned horse," a statement
that does not commit one to the existence of unicorns.[8] The alternative interpretation is called the Aristotelian interpretation, which is named for
the ancient Greek philosopher Aristotle (384–322 B.C.E.). According to the
Aristotelian interpretation, a universal categorical proposition is true only
if the subject term picks out at least one existent object. *On the Aristotelian interpretation*, a statement of the form "All *S* are *P*" claims *both*
that "All *S* are *P*" *and* that "Some *S* are *P*"; a statement of the form "No *S*
are *P*" claims *both* "No *S* are *P*" *and* "Some *S* are not *P*." So, on the Aristotelian interpretation, the proposition "All unicorns are one-horned
horses" is false since there are no unicorns. Because the Boolean interpretation separates the question of *existential import*, that is, a statement's
commitment to an object in the subject class, from universal propositions,
it allows one to make true universal claims about nonexistent objects. In
contexts in which one wants to make an existential claim about the subject,
one can explicitly make a complex claim such as, "All *S* are *P*, and there is
something that is *S*." It is for this reason that most logicians accept the
Boolean interpretation.[9]

Why bring this up? There are *some* logicians who believe that the Aristotelian interpretation is more natural or "intuitive." Assuming the Aristotelian interpretation has two consequences. (1) On the Aristotelian interpretation, there are nine additional valid inferences. They are called
conditionally valid; that is, they are valid on the condition that the subject
term picks out at least one existent thing. Users of ordinary English are often imprecise. If they *know* that the subject term of the minor premise *in
fact* picks out at least one thing, they often will *assume* the Aristotelian interpretation. (2) There are various relations among categorical propositions
that hold on the Aristotelian interpretation but *not* on the Boolean interpretation.[10]

The following nine forms are conditionally valid:

All *M* are *P*.	All *M* are *P*	All *P* are *M*.
All *S* are *M*.	All *M* are *S*.	[Some *P* are *M*.]
[Some *S* are *M*.]	[Some *M* are *S*.]	All *M* are *S*.
∴ Some *S* are *P*.	∴ Some *S* are *P*.	∴ Some *S* are *P*.

All *P* are *M*.	All *P* are *M*.	No *M* are *P*.
No *S* are *M*.	No *M* are *S*.	All *S* are *M*.
[Some *S* are not *M*.]	[Some *S* are not *M*.][11]	[Some *S* are *P*.]
∴ Some *S* are not *P*.	∴ Some *S* are not *P*.	∴ Some *S* are not *P*.

No *P* are *M*.   No *M* are *P*.   No *P* are *M*.
All *S* are *M*.   All *M* are *S*.   All *M* are *S*.
[Some *S* are *M*.]   [Some *M* are *S*.]   [Some *M* are *S*.]
∴ Some *S* are not *P*.   ∴ Some *S* are not *P*.   ∴ Some *S* are not *P*.

Notice that in each case if one substitutes the particular proposition for the universal proposition above it, the argument is valid using either the rules or Venn diagrams. Since the Aristotelian interpretation, in effect, claims that a universal proposition makes two claims, namely, *both* the universal and the particular of the same quality (affirmative or negative), you may draw whichever conclusion follows given the universal *or* the particular form of either proposition.

5.2.3 Odd Words

Two propositions are *contradictories* if the truth of one entails the falsehood of the other and vice versa. A universal affirmative proposition and a particular negative proposition with the same subject and predicate terms are contradictories, as are a universal negative proposition and a particular affirmative proposition with the same subject and predicate terms. If one is given a pair of contradictory propositions, one knows that one is true and the other is false, even if one does not know which is true. If one does know that one of a pair of contradictory propositions is true, one can immediately infer that the other is false and vice versa. The relation of contradictoriness applies to categorical propositions on both the Boolean and the Aristotelian interpretations.

On the Aristotelian interpretation of categorical propositions, there are additional relations among propositions. This is because on the Aristotelian interpretation—but *not* the Boolean interpretation— universal categorical propositions have *existential import*. A proposition has existential import if it must apply to at least one existent thing to be true. Both interpretations assume that particular propositions have existential import. The following relations apply *only* to the Aristotelian interpretation.

Two propositions are *contraries* if they can both be false, but they cannot both be true. So, if one knows that one proposition is true, one can infer that the other is false. But if one knows that one proposition is false, one *cannot* infer anything regarding the truth or falsehood of

---

(Continued)

(Continued)

---

the other. On the Aristotelian interpretation, universal affirmative propositions and universal negative propositions with the same subject and predicate terms are contraries.

Two propositions are *subcontraries* if they can both be true, but they cannot both be false. So, if one knows that one proposition is false, one can infer that the other proposition is true. But if one knows that one proposition is true, one *cannot* infer anything regarding the truth or falsehood of the other proposition. On the Aristotelian interpretation, particular affirmative propositions and particular negative propositions with the same subject and predicate terms are subcontraries.

Since on the Aristotelian interpretation universal propositions have existential import, the truth of a universal affirmative proposition entails the truth of a particular affirmative proposition, and the truth of a universal negative proposition entails the truth of a particular negative proposition. This relation is called *subalternation*.

5.3 ENTHYMEMES

Sometimes categorical syllogisms are incompletely stated. An incompletely stated argument is called an *enthymeme* or an *enthymematic argument*. Enthymemes can hide various sins. They can hide the fact that an argument form is invalid. They can also hide the fact that the unstated premise or conclusion is false. So, if a premise is unstated, one should determine *whether* there is a premise that will yield a valid syllogism, and if the conclusion is unstated, one should determine *whether* any conclusion follows from the premises. Once the missing element is found, one should determine whether the missing element is true.

If the conclusion is not stated, the following procedure will allow you to determine whether any conclusion follows from the premises, and, if so, what conclusion follows.[12]

1. Make sure the middle term is not assigned different meanings in the premises. If it is, *no* conclusion follows. (It is invalid: rule 1. Go no further.)
2. Be sure the middle term is distributed *exactly* once. If it is not, *no* conclusion follows. (The syllogism is invalid: rule 2. Go no further.)

3. Be sure there are *not* two negative premises. If there are, *no* conclusion follows. (The syllogism is invalid: rule 5. Go no further.)
4. Be sure there are *not* two particular premises. If there are, *no* conclusion follows. (The syllogism is invalid: rule 6. Go no further.)
5. If there is a *particular* premise, the conclusion also must be particular.
6. If there is a *negative* premise, the conclusion also must be negative.
7. Determine which is the major term and which is the minor term by appealing to the distribution of terms in the premises: If a term is distributed in the premise, it must also be distributed in the conclusion. If a term is undistributed in the premise, it must also be undistributed in the conclusion.

If a premise is not stated, the following procedure will allow you to determine whether any premise will yield a valid syllogism and, if so, what that premise is.

1. Be sure the term that is common to the premise and the conclusion is either distributed in both the premise and the conclusion *or* is distributed in neither the premise nor the conclusion. If the term is distributed only once, *no* premise will yield a valid conclusion. (The syllogism is invalid: rule 3 or rule 4. Go no further.)
2. Be sure that there is *not* a particular premise and a universal conclusion. If there is particular premise and a universal conclusion, *no* premise will yield a valid syllogism. (The syllogism is invalid: rule 6. Go no further.)
3. Be sure there is *not* a negative premise and an affirmative conclusion. If there is a negative premise and an affirmative conclusion, *no* premise will yield a valid syllogism. (The syllogism is invalid: rule 5. Go no further.)
4. If the conclusion is universal, the missing premise is also universal.
5. If the conclusion is particular and the given premise is also particular, the missing premise is universal.
6. If the conclusion is particular and the given premise is universal, the missing premise is particular.
7. If the term common to the missing premise and the conclusion is distributed in the conclusion, it must also be distributed in the premise. If the term is undistributed in the conclusion, it must also be undistributed in the premise.
8. If the middle term is distributed in the given premise, it must be undistributed in the missing premise. If the middle term is undistributed in the given premise, it must be distributed in the missing premise.[13]

9. Make sure each of the terms is assigned the same meaning through-out the syllogism. If they are not, the syllogism is invalid (rule 1).

Check to make sure that the missing premise or conclusion is true.

NOTES

1. In ordinary English, the complement of a class-term is often marked by the prefixes *un-*, *in-*, or *im-*. For example, the complement of the term *mortals* is *im-mortals*. But this is not always the case. For example, flammable objects are just as burnable as inflammable objects.

2. We examine other kinds of syllogisms in later chapters.

3. Standard form is a convenience but an important one. Because there is a standard form, it is possible to pick out categorical syllogisms on the basis of the kinds of propositions included together with the position of the middle term in them. This, however, is of no importance to the issues in this book.

4. There are various ways in which rules for evaluating syllogisms can be stated. Given the rules above, if one has a syllogism—if the syllogism does *not* violate rule 1—then if it violates any one of rules 2 to 6, it will violate at least two rules.

5. Technically, these fifteen are unconditionally valid. Below we'll consider nine more forms that are *conditionally* valid, that is, valid *assuming* that the minor term picks out an existent thing.

6. Some people who have no trouble diagramming an *E* proposition find dia-gramming an *A* proposition puzzling. If one remembers that an *A* proposition, "All *S* are *P*," is logically equivalent to its obverse, "No *S* are non-*P*," one can recognize that it is again a case of shading what is empty.

7. This *does not* mean there were no champions of the Boolean interpretation before Boole. René Descartes was a Boolean about 200 years before Boole. See Descartes's *Principles of Philosophy*, Part I, §10.

8. We discuss conditional statements in the next chapter.

9. In addition to statements about mythical beasts which are true by definition (but have no existential import), there are such things as scientific "idealizations" that one wants to be true but could not be true on the Aristotelian interpretation. Newton's law of inertia, for example, is an idealization since there are no objects that are not acted on by some outside force.

10. We will examine these in the "Odd Words" discussion at the end of this chapter.

11. "No *M* are *S*" is logically equivalent to its converse, "No *S* are *M*." The par-ticular proposition corresponding to the latter is "Some *S* are not *M*."

12. Alternatively, one could construct a Venn diagram to determine whether any conclusion follows from a pair of premises. The completed diagram will show you *what* conclusion follows, if any does follow.

13. If everything has been done correctly, this should happen as a matter of course. This provides a check to see whether everything has been done correctly.

6

ARGUMENTS BASED ON PROPOSITIONS

6.1 STATEMENT FORMS

The most common deductive arguments are based on relations among propositions (statements) rather than relations among classes (categories). The propositions are treated as *truth functional*: The truth of compound propositions in such arguments is wholly determined by the *truth values* (truth or falsehood) of their component propositions. We shall be concerned with five kinds of truth-functional compound statements:

- *Negation*: If a proposition is true, its negation is false.
- *Conjunction*: A conjunction is true if and only if both of its component propositions (*conjuncts*) are true.
- *Disjunction*: A disjunction is true *unless* both of its component propositions (*disjuncts*) are false.[1]
- *Material conditionality*: A conditional statement consists of two parts, the *antecedent* (*if*-clause) and the *consequent* (*then*-clause). A material conditional is true *except* when the antecedent is true and the consequent is false.[2]
- *Material equivalence*: A statement of material equivalence is true if and only if both component statements have the same truth value.

6.1.1. A Logical Digression: Symbols and Truth Table Definitions

The past century saw a revolution in logic: Logicians developed symbolic notations to represent arguments. So, there are symbols to represent negation, conjunction, disjunction, material implication, and material equivalence. The symbols are defined by *truth tables*, which are systematic arrays that show all possible combinations of truth values for the statement. Properly, the symbols mean exactly what the truth tables tell you, neither more nor less. So, we introduce symbols and their truth table definitions. In a later Logical Digression, we'll show how truth tables are used to determine whether an argument form is valid.

The symbol for negation is the tilde (~).[3] ~p is the negation of p. The *negation* of a proposition is false when the proposition is true and true when the proposition is false. The truth table for the tilde is as follows:

p	~p
T	F
F	T

Conjunction is represented by the ampersand (&).[4] A conjunction is true if and only if both conjuncts are true. The truth table for the ampersand is as follows:

p	q	$p \& q$
T	T	T
T	F	F
F	T	F
F	F	F

Weak disjunction is represented by the wedge (∨). A disjunction is true *except* when both its disjuncts are false. The truth table for the wedge is as follows:

p	q	$p \vee q$
T	T	T
T	F	T
F	T	T
F	F	F

Material conditionality is represented by the arrow (→).[5] A material conditional is true *except* when its antecedent is true and its consequent is false. The truth table for the arrow is as follows:

p q	*p → q*
T T	T
T F	F
F T	T
F F	T

Material equivalence is represented by the double arrow (↔).[6] A statement of material equivalence is true if and only if its two components have the same truth value. The truth table for the double arrow is as follows:

p q	*p ↔ q*
T T	T
T F	F
F T	F
F F	T

One should notice that, except for negation, the symbols introduced here govern statements taken two at a time. The tilde (~) governs whatever statement (regardless how complex) is to its immediate right. Since the ampersand (&), wedge (∨), arrow (→), and double arrow (↔) govern statements two at a time, we need "punctuation marks" to show which statements are governed by a given symbol. The punctuation marks in symbolic logic are called *grouping indicators*. We group statements with parentheses (()), square brackets ([]), and braces ({}). We shall see how these are employed in the discussion of argument forms.

6.2 ARGUMENT FORMS

There are ten common valid propositional argument forms. Where *p*, *q*, *r*, and *s* are statements:

Affirming the Antecedent (*modus ponens*)

If *p*, then *q*.   *p → q*
p.   Therefore, *q*.   *p* ∴ *q*

Denying the Consequent (modus tollens)

If p, then q.   p → q
Not q.   Therefore, not p.   ~q ∴ ~p

Disjunctive Syllogism

Either p or q.   p ∨ q
Not p.   Therefore, q.   ~p ∴ q

Hypothetical Syllogism

If p, then q.   p → q
If q, then r. Therefore, if p then r.   q → r ∴ p → r

Simplification

p and q.   Therefore, p.   p & q ∴ p

Conjunction

p.   p
q.   Therefore, p and q.   q ∴ p & q

Addition

p.   Therefore, p or q.   p ∴ p ∨ q

Absorption

If p then q.   Therefore, if p then both p and q.   p → ∴ p → (p & q)

Constructive Dilemma

If p then q; and if r then s.   (p → q) & (r → s)
Either p or r.   Therefore, either q or s.   p ∨ r ∴ q ∨ s

Destructive Dilemma

If p then q; and if r then s.   (p → q) & (r → s)
Either not q or not s.   ~q ∨ ~s ∴ ~p ∨ ~r
Therefore, either not p or not r.

There are two common *invalid* propositional argument forms, that is, forms in which it is possible for all the premises to be true and the conclusion to be false. Where p and q are statements:

Fallacy of Affirming the Consequent

If p, then q. $p \rightarrow q$
q.   Therefore, p. $q \therefore p$

Fallacy of Denying the Antecedent

If p, then q. $p \rightarrow q$
Not p.   Therefore, not q. $\sim p \therefore \sim q$

6.2.1 A Logical Digression: Truth Tables for Testing the Validity of Arguments

Truth tables can be used to determine whether an argument or argument form is valid. One simply constructs a diagram for each of the premises and the conclusion. Using the definitions of the symbols given in the last Logical Digression, the diagram for affirming the antecedent (*modus ponens*) is as follows:

p q	$p \rightarrow q$	p $\therefore$	q
T T	T	T	T
T F	F	T	F ✓
F T	T	F	T
F F	T	F	F ✓

A truth table provides an array of all possible combinations of truth values for all the statements in the argument. Thus, it allows one to determine whether there is a combination in which all the premises are true and the conclusion is false. In the second line of the truth table, the first premise is false. In the fourth line of the truth table, the second premise is false. Thus, there is no combination of truth values such that all the premises are true and the conclusion is false. Thus, affirming the antecedent is a valid form.

The following truth tables show that denying the consequent (*modus tollens*), disjunctive syllogism, hypothetical syllogism, simplification, conjunction, and addition are valid argument forms. Notice that the number of rows in the truth table doubles with the addition of each additional simple statement in the syllogism. In general, the number of rows in a truth table equals 2^n, where n is the number of simple statements in the argument.

Denying the Consequent (modus tollens)

p q	$p \rightarrow q$	$\sim q$	$\therefore$	$\sim p$
T T	T	F		F ✓
T F	F	T		F ✓
F T	T	F		T
F F	T	T		T

Disjunctive Syllogism

p q	$p \vee q$	$\sim p$	$\therefore$	q
T T	T	F		T
T F	T	F		F ✓
F T	T	T		T
F F	F	T		F ✓

Hypothetical Syllogism

p q r	$p \rightarrow q$	$q \rightarrow r$	$\therefore$ $p \rightarrow r$
T T T	T	T	T
T T F	T	F	F ✓
T F T	F	T	T
T F F	F	T	F ✓
F T T	T	T	T
F T F	T	F	T
F F T	T	T	T
F F F	T	T	T

Simplification

p q	p & q	p
T T	T	T
T F	F	T
F T	F	F ✓
F F	F	F ✓

Conjunction

p q	p	q	∴	p & q
T T	T	T		T
T F	T	F		F ✓
F T	F	T		F ✓
F F	F	F		F ✓

Addition

p q	p	∴	p ∨ q
T T	T		T
T F	T		T
F T	F		T
F F	F		F ✓

When one constructs a truth table for compound statements, one must construct columns for each of the component statements. So, the truth tables for absorption, constructive dilemma, and destructive dilemma include columns for component propositions. *These are included* only *so that one can construct a column for the entire premise.* A line is drawn through them to indicate that they are *not* taken into account in determining the validity of the argument.

Absorption

p q	p → q	∴ p → (p & q)
T T	T	T T
T F	F	F ✓ F
F T	T	T F
F F	T	T F

Constructive Dilemma

p q r s	$(p \rightarrow q)$ & $(r \rightarrow s)$			$p \vee r$	$\therefore \quad q \vee s$
T T T T	T	T	T	T	T
T T T F	T	F	F	T	T
T T F T	T	T	T	T	T
T T F F	T	T	T	T	T
T F T T	F	F	T	T	T
T F T F	F	F	F	T	F ✓
T F F T	F	F	T	T	T
T F F F	F	F	T	T	F ✓
F T T T	T	T	T	T	T
F T T F	T	F	F	T	T
F T F T	T	T	T	F	T
F T F F	T	T	T	F	T
F F T T	T	T	T	T	T
F F T F	T	F	F	T	F ✓
F F F T	T	T	T	F	T
F F F F	T	T	T	F	F ✓

Destructive Dilemma

p q r s	$(p \rightarrow q)$ & $(r \rightarrow s)$			$\sim q \vee \sim s$			$\therefore \quad \sim p \vee \sim r$		
T T T T	T	T	T	F	F	F	F	F	F ✓
T T T F	T	F	F	F	T	T	F	F	F ✓
T T F T	T	T	T	F	F	F	F	T	T
T T F F	T	T	T	F	T	T	F	T	T
T F T T	F	F	T	T	T	F	F	F	F ✓
T F T F	F	F	F	T	T	T	F	F	F ✓
T F F T	F	F	T	T	T	F	F	T	T
T F F F	F	F	T	T	T	T	F	T	T
F T T T	T	T	T	F	F	F	T	T	F
F T T F	T	F	F	F	T	T	T	T	F
F T F T	T	T	T	F	F	F	T	T	T
F T F F	T	T	T	F	T	T	T	T	T
F F T T	T	T	T	T	T	F	T	T	F
F F T F	T	F	F	T	T	T	T	T	F
F F F T	T	T	T	T	T	F	T	T	T
F F F F	T	T	T	T	T	T	T	T	T

If an argument or argument form is invalid, its truth table contains at least one row in which all the premises are true and the conclusion is false. The truth table for the fallacy of denying the antecedent is as follows (the row in which all the premises are true and the conclusion is false is circled):

$p\ q$	$p \to q$	$\sim p$ ∴	$\sim q$
T T	T	F	F ✓
T F	F	F	T
F T	T	T	F ✓
F F	T	T	T

The truth table for the fallacy of affirming the consequent is as follows:

$p\ q$	$p \to q$	q ∴	p
T T	T	T	T
T F	F	F	T
F T	T	T	F ✓
F F	T	F	F ✓

6.2.2 Odd Words: Tautology, Contradiction, Contingent Statement

A *tautology* is a statement that is true in virtue of its logical form. A *contradiction* is a statement that is false in virtue of its logical form. A *contingent statement* is statement that is *neither* true nor false in virtue of its logical form. One can determine whether a statement form is a tautology, a contradiction, or a contingent statement by constructing a truth table.

Consider the truth table for the statement form $p \lor \sim p$:

p	$p \lor \sim p$
T	T F
F	T T

(Continues)

(Continued)

Since every truth value under $p \lor \sim p$ is true, the statement form is a tautology.

Consider a truth table for $p \mathbin{\&} \sim p$:

p	$p \mathbin{\&} \sim p$	
T	F	F
F	F	T

Since every truth value under $p \mathbin{\&} \sim p$ is false, the statement form is a contradiction.

The definitions for each of the symbols we introduced ($\&$, $\lor$, $\rightarrow$, and $\leftrightarrow$) show that each of those statements is contingent, as are all simple statements. For example, the definition of the arrow ($\rightarrow$) is:

p q	$p \rightarrow q$
T T	T
T F	F
F T	T
F F	T

Two statement forms are *logically equivalent* if they have the same truth values for any assignment of truth values for their simple propositions. Whether two statements are logically equivalent can be determined by a truth table. For example, if one constructs truth tables for the forms $p \rightarrow q$ and $\sim p \lor q$, one discovers that the two statement forms are logically equivalent:

p q	$p \rightarrow q$	$\sim p \lor q$	
T T	T	F	T
T F	F	F	F
F T	T	T	T
F F	T	F	T

If two statement forms are logically equivalent, then a biconditional in which each statement is a component—when the two statements

flank a double arrow—is a tautological statement of material equiva-
lence. So, the statement form $(p \rightarrow q) \leftrightarrow (\sim p \vee q)$ is a tautology:

p q	$(p \rightarrow q) \leftrightarrow (\sim p \vee q)$
T T	T T F T
T F	F T F F
F T	T T T T
F F	T T T T

We introduce the symbol $\leftarrow L \rightarrow$ to represent logical equivalence.[7]
So, the statement $(p \rightarrow q) \leftarrow L \rightarrow (\sim p \vee q)$ indicates that $p \rightarrow q$ is logically equivalent to $\sim p \vee q$.

6.3 LOGICAL EQUIVALENCES

Two propositions are logically equivalent if they are both true or both false
given the same assignment of truth values to their component propositions.
If one is doing symbolic logic, these equivalences are sometimes necessary
to show that a conclusion follows from a set of premises. If one is proceed-
ing less formally, one still needs consideration of these equivalences to assure oneself that some of the statements in an argument are logically equivalent, that is, to assure oneself that the truth of the premises shows that the
conclusion is true.[8]

Commutation

$(p \mathbin{\&} q) \leftarrow L \rightarrow (q \mathbin{\&} p)$
$(p \vee q) \leftarrow L \rightarrow (q \vee p)$

The order of conjuncts in a conjunction and disjuncts in a disjunction
does not affect the truth value of the statement. This is called commutation.
So, a statement of the form p and q is logically equivalent to a statement of
the form q and p, and a statement of the form p or q is logically equivalent
to q or p.

Association

$[p \mathbin{\&} (q \mathbin{\&} r)] \leftarrow L \rightarrow [(p \mathbin{\&} q) \mathbin{\&} r]$
$[p \vee (q \vee r)] \leftarrow L \rightarrow [(p \vee q) \vee r]$

Conjunctions and disjunctions group statements two at a time. If you have a conjunction composed of three conjuncts or a disjunction composed of three disjuncts, moving the grouping indicators has no effect on the statement's truth value. So, a statement of the form p & $(q$ & $r)$ is logically equivalent to a statement of the form $(p$ & $q)$ & r; and a statement of the form $p \vee (q \vee r)$ is logically equivalent to a statement of the form $(p \vee q) \vee r$.

Distribution

$[p$ & $(q \vee r)] \leftarrow L\rightarrow [(p$ & $q) \vee (p$ & $r)]$
$[p \vee (q$ & $r)] \leftarrow L\rightarrow [(p \vee q)$ & $(p \vee r)]$

A statement conjoined to a disjunction is logically equivalent to a statement composed of a conjunction of the first conjunct with the first disjunct disjoined to the first conjunct conjoined to the second disjunct. A statement disjoined to a conjunction is logically equivalent to a statement composed of the first disjunct disjoined with the first conjunct conjoined with a disjunction of the first disjunct and the second conjunct.

DeMorgan's Theorems

$\sim(p$ & $q) \leftarrow L\rightarrow (\sim p \vee \sim q)$
$\sim(p \vee q) \leftarrow L\rightarrow (\sim p$ & $\sim q)$

The negation of a disjunction is logically equivalent to a conjunction of the negations of the original statement's disjuncts. The negation of a conjunction is logically equivalent to the disjunction of the negations of the original statement's conjuncts.

Double Negation

$p \leftarrow L\rightarrow \sim\sim p$

Any proposition is logically equivalent to the double negation of that statement.

Transposition

$(p \rightarrow q) \leftarrow L\rightarrow (\sim q \rightarrow \sim p)$

A conditional statement of the form "If p, then q" is logically equivalent to a statement of the form "If not q, then not p."

Material Implication

$(p \rightarrow q) \leftarrow L \rightarrow (\sim p \vee q)$

A conditional statement of the form "If p, then q" is logically equivalent to a disjunction of the form "Either not p or q."

Material Equivalence

$(p \leftrightarrow q) \leftarrow L \rightarrow [(p \rightarrow q) \,\&\, (q \rightarrow p)]$
$(p \leftrightarrow q) \leftarrow L \rightarrow [(p \,\&\, q) / (\sim p \,\&\, \sim q)]$

A statement of the form "p if and only if q" is logically equivalent to a statement of the form "If p then q, and if q then p." A statement of the form "p if and only if q" is also logically equivalent to a statement of the form "Either both p and q, or both not p and not q."

Exportation

$[p \rightarrow (q \rightarrow r)] \leftarrow L \rightarrow [(p \,\&\, q) \rightarrow r]$

A statement of the form "If p, then if q then r" is logically equivalent to a statement of the form "If both p and q, then r."

Tautology

$p \leftarrow L \rightarrow (p \,\&\, p)$
$p \leftarrow L \rightarrow (p \vee p)$

Any statement is logically equivalent to a conjunction of that statement with itself. Any statement is logically equivalent to a disjunction of that statement with itself.

6.3.1 A Logical Digression: Demonstrating the Equivalences with Truth Tables

As we noticed in the previous Odd Words section, two statements are logically equivalent if and only if a truth table for a statement of material equivalence with the two statements as components is a tautology. In this Logical Digression, we construct a truth table for each of the logical equivalences above, showing that each is a tautological statement of material equivalence.

Commutation

p q	(p & q) ↔ (q & p)	(p ∨ q) ↔ (q ∨ p)
T T	T T T	T T T
T F	F T F	T T T
F T	F T F	T T T
F F	F T F	F T F

Association

p q r	[p & (q & r)] ↔ [(p & q) & r]	[p ∨ (q ∨ r)] ↔ [(p ∨ q) ∨ r]
T T T	T T T T T	T T T T T
T T F	F F T T F	T T T T T
T F T	F F T F F	T T T T T
T F F	F F T F F	T F T T T
F T T	F T T F F	T T T T T
F T F	F F T F F	T T T T T
F F T	F F T F F	T T T F T
F F F	F F T F F	F F T F F

Distribution

p q r	[p & (q ∨ r)] ↔ [(p & q) ∨ (p & r)]
T T T	T T T T T T
T T F	T T T T T F
T F T	T T T F T T
T F F	F F T F F F
F T T	F T T F F F
F T F	F T T F F F
F F T	F T T F F F
F F F	F F T F F F

p q r	[p	∨	(q & r)]	↔	[(p ∨ q)	&	(p ∨ r)]
T T T		T	T	T		T	T
T T F		T	F	T		T	T
T F T		T	F	T		T	T
T F F		T	F	T		T	T
F T T		T	T	T		T	T
F T F		F	F	T		F	F
F F T		F	F	T	F	F	T
F F F		F	F	T		F	F

DeMorgan's Theorems

p q	~(p	&	q)	↔	(~p	∨	~q)	~(p	∨	q)	↔	(~p	&	~q)
T T	F	T		T	F	F	F	F	T		T	F	F	F
T F	T	F		T	F	T	T	F	T		T	F	F	T
F T	T	F		T	T	T	F	F	T		T	T	F	F
F F	T	F		T	T	T	T	T	F		T	T	T	T

Double Negation

p	p	↔	~	~p
T	T	T	T	F
F	F	T	F	T

Transposition

p q	(p → q)	↔	(~q	→	~p)
T T	T	T	F	T	F
T F	F	T	T	F	F
F T	T	T	F	T	T
F F	T	T	T	T	T

Material Implication

p q	(p → q) ↔ (~p ∨ q)
T T	T T F T
T F	F T F F
F T	T T T T
F F	T T T T

Material Equivalence

p q	(p ↔ q) ↔ [(p → q) & (q → p)]
T T	T T T T T
T F	F T F F T
F T	F T T F F
F F	T T T T T

p q	(p ↔ q) ↔ [(p & q) ∨ (~p & ~q)]
T T	T T T T F F F
T F	F T F F F F T
F T	F T F F T F F
F F	T T F T T T T

Exportation

p q r	[p → (q → r)] ↔ [(p & q) → r]
T T T	T T T T T
T T F	F F T T F
T F T	T T T F T
T F F	T T T F T
F T T	T T T F T
F T F	T F T F T
F F T	T T T F T
F F F	T T T F T

Tautology

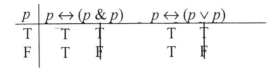

NOTES

1. This is known as *weak* or *inclusive* disjunction. In the case of weak disjunction, if one is given that one disjunct is false, it follows that the other is true. If one is given that one disjunct is true, you can make no inferences about the other disjunct. This is contrasted with *strong* or *exclusive* disjunction, which claims that either one disjunct or the other is true and that they are not both true. Exclusive disjunction is common on restaurant menus.

2. Material conditionals are not the only type of conditional statements. Material conditionals are concerned only about the relationships between the truth values of propositions. For example, they make no causal claims, as some conditionals do. Nonetheless, this interpretation of the conditional statement works extremely well for discussing argument forms.

3. The choice of symbols is somewhat arbitrary. Some logicians use the bar (-). Others use the hook (¬). Still others place a bar over the statement to be negated (p̄).

4. Some logicians use the dot (·) or the caret (ˆ).

5. Some logicians use the horseshoe (⊃).

6. Some logicians use the tribar (≡).

7. Some authors represent this by $\underset{\equiv}{\text{T}}$.

8. Once we have these equivalences, we have a *complete* system of propositional logic. This will allow one to construct what logicians call proofs; that is, for any valid argument in propositional logic, it allows one to provide a finite series of statements showing that the conclusion follows from the premises, given the ten valid argument forms and the equivalences introduced in this section.

7

PROBABILITY CALCULATIONS

While a valid argument with true premises allows one to be certain that the conclusion is true, a cogent inductive argument provides only some probability that its conclusion is true. Some probability calculations, however, are strictly deductive.

When statisticians talk about probability calculations, they state probability on a scale from zero to one: one implies certainty that an event *will* happen, and zero implies certainty that an event *will not* happen. We often talk informally in terms of percentages. "There is a 90% probability that x will occur in circumstances y" is properly stated as "There is a probability of .9 that x will occur in circumstances y."

7.1 THEORIES OF PROBABILITY

There are two theories of probability.[1] These theories concern the *source* of one's data. The formulae for calculating probabilities are the same regardless of the theory. The *relative frequency theory* is based on empirically known statistics. Assume that Fred is forty and wants to know the probability that he will live to eighty. Checking a standard mortality table,[2] one discovers that 95,377 out of 100,000 males born are still alive at age forty. By age eighty, there are only 43,564. Using the formula

$$P(A) = \frac{f}{n}$$

we divide the frequency at eighty (f) by the frequency at forty (n) to determine the probability that Fred will live to be eighty:

$$\frac{43,564}{95,377} = .446755822$$

The subjective theory is based on one's individual beliefs. On it, probability is one's degree of confidence in a particular proposition. Subjective theories exist on a continuum. On some, that degree of confidence need not have anything to do with real-world facts. On others, that degree of confidence is supposed to be only relative to one's available evidence. If a bookie gives the odds of five to four in favor of one's favorite team in the next game, one divides the favorable outcomes (five) by all possible outcomes (nine) and concludes that the probability that one's team will win is .545556 (or 54.5556%).

7.1.1 Odd Words: Relative Frequency and Subjective Theories

There is a sense in which the distinction between relative frequency theories and subjective theories is not exhaustive. There is a sense in which the distinction is one of degree rather than kind.

Relative frequency theories typically refer to statistical surveys. Such surveys are never completely accurate. When dealing with census data, one knows that not every resident of the country on a certain date completed the census form. Actuarial tables are out of date as soon as they are published, and some deaths have almost certainly gone unreported. Nonetheless, typically a confidence level (or confidence interval) is ascribed to the survey that resulted in the data. For example, the U.S. Census Bureau ascribes a 90% confidence level for to its state and county estimates.[3] This means that, based on long experience, they believe their data are correct 90% of the time.[4]

The subjective theory, in an extreme version, is merely the degree of certainty one ascribes to one's belief. This belief might be informed or uninformed. If the degree of certainty is informed by past experience, some would suggest it is not *purely* subjective. Hence, some suggest that the relative frequency/subjective distinction is not exhaustive. In fact, on versions of the subjective theory that lie on the other extreme, probability is a measure of the *appropriate* degree of

belief given the available evidence. And that relation is a purely objective one. Thus, what subjective theories have in common is that
they are based on degrees of belief. They are all subjective in that
sense. Those that emphasize that degree being based on the available
evidence are not "subjective" in the other sense of the word (not being based on facts or evidence).

   If there is a significant difference between the relative frequency
and subjective theories, it is that relative frequencies can be determined regarding *countable* things. The certainty of the data that provides the basis for the calculations, however, like the certainty ascribed by subjective theories, is less than perfect. In terms of
certainty, the differences between the theories is a matter of degree.

7.2 RULES OF PROBABILITY

The *restricted conjunction rule* allows one to calculate the probability that
two or more independent events occur. Events are independent if the occurrence of one event has no effect on the probability that another event
will occur. For example, each tossing of a single coin is an independent
event. Where $A, B, \ldots N$ are independent events,

$P(A \text{ and } B \text{ and } \ldots \text{ and } N) = P(A) \times P(B) \times \ldots \times P(N)$

So, the probability of throwing heads in two successive tosses of a fair coin
is 1/4:

$P(H_1 \text{ and } H_2) = \dfrac{1}{2} \times \dfrac{1}{2} = \dfrac{1}{4} = .25$

The probability of throwing heads on three successive tosses of a fair coin
is 1/8:

$P(H_1 \text{ and } H_2 \text{ and } H_3) = \dfrac{1}{2} \times \dfrac{1}{2} \times \dfrac{1}{2} = \dfrac{1}{8} = .125$

The *general conjunction rule* is used to calculate the probability of two or
more events when the events are dependent on one another. Two events are
dependent when the outcome of one event affects the probability of the
second event.

   $P(A \text{ and } B \text{ and } \ldots \text{ and } N) = P(A) \times P(B \text{ given } A) \times \ldots \times P(N \text{ given } A$
through $N - 1)$

For example, if you want to determine the chances of successively drawing red queens from a standard poker deck, the formula would be

$$\frac{2}{52} \times \frac{1}{51} = \frac{2}{2652} = \frac{1}{1326} = 0.000754$$

If one is playing Powerball, one's objective is to pick the numbers of five out of fifty-five white balls "the order makes no difference" plus the red powerball out of forty-two possibilities. The formula is

$$\frac{5}{55} \times \frac{4}{54} \times \frac{3}{53} \times \frac{2}{52} \times \frac{1}{51} \times \frac{1}{42} = \frac{120}{17532955440} = \frac{1}{146107962}$$

If the order *did* make a difference, then there would be only once chance of being correct in each successive draw:

$$\frac{1}{55} \times \frac{1}{54} \times \frac{1}{53} \times \frac{1}{52} \times \frac{1}{51} \times \frac{1}{42} = \frac{1}{17532955440}$$

If one is concerned with the probability that one of two or more possible events will occur, one adds probabilities. The *restricted disjunction rule* concerns mutually exclusive events (the occurrence of one event precludes the occurrence of the other).

$$P(A \text{ or } B \text{ or} \ldots \text{or } N) = P(A) + P(B) + \ldots + P(N)$$

If one were concerned with the probability of rolling either a four or a six with a fair die, the formula would be

$$P(4 \text{ or } 6) = \frac{1}{6} + \frac{1}{6} = \frac{1}{3} = .3334$$

The *general disjunction rule* allows one to calculate the probability that either of two or more independent events will occur:

$$P(A \text{ or } B \text{ or} \ldots \text{or } N) = \{[P(A) + P(B) + \ldots P(N)] - [P(A \times B \times \ldots \times N)]\}$$

For example, assume that there is a probability of .63 that Aunt Tillie will live to be eighty and a probability of .52 that Uncle George will live to be eighty. The probability that either Aunt Tillie or Uncle George will live to be eighty is

$P(T \text{ or } G) = [(.63 + .52) - (.63 \times .52)] = (1.15 - 0.3276) = 0.8224$

The *negation rule* tells one the probability that an event will occur given the probability that it *will not* occur:

$P(A) = 1 - P(\text{not-}A)$

If one is given that there is a probability of .65 that the football team will lose, it follows that there is a probability of .35 that the team will win.

Conditional probability[5]
Where $P(B|A)$ is understood as the probability of B given A,

$$P(B|A) = \frac{P(A \& B)}{P(A)}$$

If one has drawn a face card from a fresh full deck of cards, what is the probability that it is a king? This is the conditional probability of drawing a king given that one has drawn a face card. In this case, P(Draw a face card & Draw a king) is 4/52. And P(Draw a face card) is 12/52. Thus, P(Draw a king | Draw a face card) = 4/52 divided by 12/52, which turns out to be 1/3.

Bayes's Theorem

$$P(A|B) = \frac{P(B|A) \times P(A)}{P(B)}$$

This is often stated in terms of the probability of a hypothesis (H) given certain observations (O):

$$P(H|O) = \frac{P(O|H) \times P(H)}{P(O)}$$

$P(H|O)$ refers to the probability of hypothesis H conditioned on evidence (or observation) O and is also often termed the *posterior probability* of H since it refers to H's probability after one takes into account O. By contrast, $P(H)$ and $P(O)$ refer to the probability of H apart from O (not conditioned on *O*) and the probability of *O* apart from *H* (not conditioned on *H*). This is *not* the probability of *H* or *O* given all evidence (since that would include both) or the probability of *H* given not-*O* (or *O* given not-*H*) but the probability of *H* or *O* regardless of other information. For this reason, *P(H)* is often called the *prior probability* of *H* since it refers to *H*'s probability without taking *O* into account. The *P(O|H)* refers to the probability of *O* on the assumption that *H* is true. That is, if *H* were true, it is the probability *O* would be true. It is the probability that the hypothesis would (if true) result in the relevant evidence/observation. This is *not* the same as the probability of *H* on the assumption of *O* (which refers to how probable the hypothesis is, given the evidence/observation). And *P(O|H)* is often termed the *likelihood* of *H*.

Suppose that Calvin is being tested to see if he has a particular disease and tests positive. The test is 99.9% accurate (i.e., the probability that he will test positive if he has the disease is 0.999) and the overall rate of the disease in his demographic category is 1 in 2000 (i.e., probability is 0.0005). How probable is it that he has the disease given the positive result? This can be solved with Bayes's theorem. *P*(positive result | has the disease) is 0.999. *P*(has the disease) is the probability that he has the disease independent of any other information, which is the overall background rate of the disease for people in his demographic group, which is 0.0005. *P*(tests positive) will be the probability that he tests positive regardless of any other information, which is the probability of testing positive whether or not he has the disease. Thus, that is the probability that he tests positive if he has the disease (0.999) times the background probability that he has the disease (0.0005) plus the probability that he tests positive if does not have the disease (0.001) times the background probability that he does not have the disease (0.9995). So, *P*(tests positive) is 0.999 × 0.0005 + 0.001 × 0.9995, which is 0.001499. Therefore, the probability that he has the disease given that he tests positive will be

$$P(H \mid O) = \frac{0.999 \ \times \ 0.0005}{0.001499}$$

This turns out to be approximately 0.33, or 33%. Thus, even though the test is 99.9% accurate, the rate of the disease is so low in the population that there is about a one-third chance he has the disease.

NOTES

1. The classical theory of probability is the relative frequency theory in those cases in which all the probabilities are equal, as in the case of throwing a fair die.

2. These statistics are drawn from the Periodic Life Table updated June 27, 2006, http://www.ssa.gov/OACT/STATS/table4c6.html, 3/5/07.

3. http://ask.census.gov/cgi-bin/askcensus.cfg/php/enduser/std_adp.php?p _faqid=530&p_created=1087842359&p_sid=qpiJAOvi&p_accessibility=0&p _redirect=&p_lva=&p_sp=cF9zcmNoPTEmcF9zb3J0X2J5PSZwX2dyaWRzb3J0PSZ wX3Jvd19jbnQ9MTA5JnBfcHJvZHM9JnBfY2F0cz0mcF9wdj0mcF9jdj0mcF9wY Wdl PTEmcF9zZWFyY2hfdGV4dD0iY29uZmlkZW5jZSBsZXZlbCI°&p_li=&p _topview=1 3/5/07.

4. See section 8.1.1 in chapter 8 for more on surveys.

5. There are two different ways to put the axioms and theorems of probability theory based on whether one takes categorical or conditional probabilities to be fundamental. A *categorical* probability is the probability of something not condi- tioned on anything else, such as $P(A)$. By contrast, a *conditional* probability is the probability of something conditioned on something else, such as $P(A|B)$. On the ap- proach used here, categorical probabilities are fundamental, and conditional prob- abilities are defined in terms of them (as described). However, on another ap- proach, conditional probabilities are fundamental, and all categorical probabilities become conditional ones. For example, they might become the probability of some- thing given only necessary (logical) truths.

8

GENERALIZATIONS AND PARTICULARIZATIONS

The structure of a valid deductive argument guarantees that if the premises are true, then the conclusion is also true. So, in an invalid argument, there is always some possibility that the premises are true and the conclusion is false. Arguments of this kind are inductive (see section 2.1.2 in chapter 2). Inductive arguments are assessed in terms of their *strength*, which, unlike validity, comes in degrees. This and the following six chapters describe several kinds of inductive arguments and the principles used to evaluate them.

8.I GENERALIZATION ARGUMENTS

In an inductive generalization, one infers that all (or some percentage) of the members of a group have a particular characteristic on the basis of a subset of that group having that characteristic. For example, I might infer that all swans are white because all the swans I have observed are white. The group (swans) is called the *overall population*, and the subset (swans I have observed) is the *sample*. Such inferences are *generalization* arguments and have the following structure:

Form of Generalization Arguments
Where *n* is a number between 0 and 100, *x* is kind of thing, and *P* is some property or relationship:

1. *n* percent of sampled *x*'s have P^1.
2. Thus, *n** percent of *x*'s have *P* (where *n** is less than or equal to *n*).

So, one might reason that since 99% of sampled swans are white, 99% of all swans are white. Alternatively, one might infer that since 60% of the sampled voters approve of Senator Smith, most voters approve of Senator Smith.

Since the sample will always be smaller than the overall population, one can never be certain what percentage of the overall population has the property in question. However, one's inference can have varying degrees of strength. And one can take steps to increase that strength. First, stronger generalizations are more modest. The *modesty* of the conclusion is based on how close the percentage of cases claimed to have *P* is to the percentage of cases in the sample that have *P*. If all the swans one has observed are white, then it would be more modest (and so a stronger inference) to claim only that most swans are white instead of claiming that all swans are white (which actually turns out to be false). Second, stronger generalizations have larger samples. If one has observed thousands of swans, that makes the inference stronger than if one has only observed hundreds. Third, stronger generalizations have more diverse samples. A sample is *diverse* on the basis of the number of differences between its members. In the case of swans, this might involve the age of the swans, the size of the swans, the gender of the swans, the geographic place they were observed, the time they were observed, and so on. And fourth, stronger generalizations have more representative samples. A sample is *representative* on the basis of the extent to which the differences between the members of the sample are in proportion to those in the overall population. So, since most (overall) swans do not live in South America, if most of one's observed swans also do not come from South America, then the inference will be a stronger one.

Principle for Evaluating Generalization Arguments
A generalization argument is *strong* the extent to which:

a. The sample population is representative of the overall population (where "representative" is the degree that, for all properties Q, the percentage of *x*'s in the sample that have Q is close to the percentage of *x*'s in the overall population that have Q).

b. The sample population is diverse (where "diversity" is the number of differences in properties among the sampled x's).

c. The sample population is larger.

d. The conclusion is more modest (where "modesty" is the extent to which the percentage n^* is less than the percentage n).

Our first generalizations about a population are not likely to be based on samples that are known to be representative. We typically know only some of the characteristics of the overall population because of previous generalizations. In such cases, the strength of these inferences will be based more on size, diversity, and modesty and less on being representative. As such, they are limited in how strong they can be. On the other hand, once a population is well known and it becomes easier to determine a sample's representativeness, diversity *per se* becomes less important. Instead, what will matter is diversity relative to those properties that are known to make a difference to the property being inferred. For example, what is representative of the American population for purposes of assessing the popularity of a politician is not necessarily the same as it would be for purposes of assessing the popularity of a clothing store. For example, a person's being over 6 feet 4 inches tall may affect their attitude toward clothing stores yet not affect their attitude toward politicians. Thus, a political pollster might rightly ignore whether their sample has (proportionally) more people over 6 feet 4 inches tall than in the overall population. But a clothing store pollster might need to be careful about this. Ultimately, stronger generalization arguments have samples that are representative of the properties that are relevant to whether x's have P.

Whether a property (such as race, gender, or height) is relevant to the property being inferred in the generalization (such as attitudes toward a politician or a clothing store) will depend on the extent to which those properties are connected. There are two ways one might try to capture this notion. The first focuses on whether having the first property has any effect on the probability of having the second property. For example, does being a woman make one more or less likely to have certain political views? If it does make a difference, then gender is relevant to assessing political attitudes. The other possibility is to speak of whether having the first property is the sort of thing that would be explained by having the second. For example, being a woman might partly explain why one has certain views about political issues.

Principle for Evaluating whether a Property Is Relevant to a Sample's Being Representative

A property *Q* is *relevant* to whether *x*'s have *P* if and only if

an *x*'s having (or not having) *Q* increases or decreases the probability of that *x*'s having *P*
or
an *x*'s having (or not having) *Q* is part of the explanation of why an *x* has (or does not have) *P*

8.1.1 A Logical Digression: Surveys and Opinion Polls

A survey or poll or census is an inductive generalization that provides a snapshot of a situation at a given time. All the criteria for generalizations apply to surveys. Insofar as the distribution of the relevant groups in the sample *does not* reflect the distribution of the same groups in the population, a survey is said to be *biased*. Insofar as everyone in the population sampled has an equal chance of being included in the sample, the survey is *random*. To the extent that a survey is random, one has good reason to believe that it is diverse in the relevant ways.[2]

Professional polling organizations often base conclusions regarding the population of the United States on a sample of 1000 people. Typically, they randomly choose telephone numbers to call. Assume their question is "Do you approve of the president's policies?" Let us say the result is that 510 of the 1000 surveyed approve of the president's policies. Their report is based on past experience. Typically a professional poll has a 95% *confidence level*: this concerns the accuracy of the poll. It is also presented with a *margin of error*: this shows the range above or below the reported percentage that experience indicates the actual approval falls. So, the results of the poll would be that 51%, ± 4%, approve of the president's policies. This means that the organization is 95% confident that between 47% and 55% of Americans approve of the president's policies.[3]

8.2 PARTICULARIZATION ARGUMENTS

Inductive particularizations run in the opposite direction from generalizations. They infer that a subset of a group has some characteristic on the basis of (a percentage of) the group having that same characteristic. So, if one begins with the claim that 99% of swans are white, then one might conclude that since Sally is a swan, Sally is probably also white. Or, if 60% of the voters approve of Senator Smith and Vic is a voter, then Vic probably also approves of Senator Smith. Such inferences are *particularization arguments* and have the following structure:

Form of Particularization Arguments
Where *n* is a number between 0 and 100, *x* is kind of thing, and P is some property or relationship:

1. *n* percent of *x*'s have P.
2. A is an *x*.
3. Thus, there is an *n** percent probability that A has P (where *n** is less than or equal to *n*).

Strong generalization arguments have sample populations that are representative of the overall population, and a strong particularization has a sample population that is representative of the individual member of the population in the conclusion. For example, if Sally is an Australian swan (which are more likely to be nonwhite than those from the rest of the world), then the sample population will have to have a larger percentage of Australian swans than if Sally were from Europe. So, the standards of a strong particularization argument run as follows:

Principle for Evaluating Particularization Arguments
A particularization argument is *strong* to the extent that:

a. The sample population is representative of the individual in question (where "representative" is the degree that, for all properties Q of A, the percentage of *x*'s that have Q is high).
b. The size of the sample population is larger.
c. The conclusion is more modest (where "modesty" is the extent to which the percentage *n** is less than the percentage *n*).

NOTES

1. For the sake of simplicity, the variable P (and later Q) is used to stand for either a property or a relation that x might have. While properties and relations are different (on most views), some attempt has been made to simplify the criteria for ease of reading.

2. Randomness is an ideal. One can never assume that the distribution of the relevant groups in the sample correlates perfectly with the same groups in the population.

3. To view the Gallup Organization's margin of error chart, see Daniel E. Flage, *The Art of Questioning: An Introduction to Critical Thinking* (Upper Saddle River, N.J.: Prentice Hall, 2004), 290. Polling organizations use *probability (random) sampling models*. Research in the natural and social sciences often use *purposive sampling models*. For a discussion of purposive sampling models, see Flage, *The Art of Questioning*, 285–87.

9

ANALOGICAL ARGUMENTS

9.1 ANALOGICAL ARGUMENTS

Steve is considering purchasing a high-definition optical disc player. He has a choice between two incompatible competing formats: HD-DVD and Blu-Ray. However, he is worried because he has heard that when videotapes began emerging in the late 1970s and early 1980s, there were also two incompatible competing formats: Betamax and VHS. He recalls his parents saying that they once bought an expensive Betamax player, only to have it become obsolete a few years later when VHS came to dominate the market. Steve concludes that the same thing will occur with HD-DVD and Blu-Ray: one will soon make the other obsolete. He decides to wait.

Steve's inference employs an analogy. Analogies make comparisons between two or more things. In this case, he is comparing the competition between HD-DVD and Blu-Ray to the competition between Betamax and VHS. *Analogical arguments* have the following structure:

Form of Analogical Arguments
1. Objects x, y, z . . . *all have properties* P, Q, R, S . . .
2. Object w *also has properties* Q, R, S . . .
3. Thus, (probably) object w *also has* P.

For a different example, someone might reason that since Andrew, Audra, and Susan are all philosophy majors, blonde, and lovers of classical music and since Andrew and Audra enjoy ballroom dancing, then Susan also enjoys ballroom dancing. In this analogy, Andrew and Audra are the *analogs* (the objects that have all the properties being compared), and Susan is the *subject* (the object compared with the analogs and inferred to have some property). Being philosophy majors, blonde, and lovers of classical music are the *basis* (the properties in common to both subject and analogs). And enjoying ballroom dancing is the *inferred property*. Returning to Steve's inference, the subject is the HD-DVD/Blu-Ray competition, and the analog is the Betamax/VHS competition. The basis of the analogy is a competition between incompatible data storage formats. And the inferred property is that one format will eventually render the other obsolete.

A number of factors are involved in evaluating an analogical argument. First, stronger analogical arguments have *more analogs*. So, if it could be said that Austin and Andrea are also blonde, philosophy majors, lovers of classical music, and enjoy ballroom dancing, then the argument that Susan enjoys ballroom dancing becomes stronger. Steve could also bolster his argument by bringing in a further analog involving incompatible competing data formats (such as the 8-track/compact cassette competition). Second, stronger analogical arguments have *more similarities* between the subject and analogs and *fewer dissimilarities* between the subject and analogs. Hence, if Andrew, Audra, and Susan were also all fans of ballet, then the inference becomes stronger. In addition, the fact that Andrew is male but Susan is female weakens the argument. In Steve's argument, if it could be shown (for example) that it is plausible for a marketable device to read both HD-DVD and Blu-Ray, that would weaken his argument (since that was not plausible in the Betamax/VHS or 8-track/compact cassette competition). Third, stronger analogical arguments have *more relevance in their similarities* and *less relevance in their dissimilarities*. Hence, the fact that Audra and Susan are both blonde is not (likely) to be important to assessing whether Susan likes ballroom dancing. By contrast, their both liking classical music is more likely to be important. (It will be left to the reader to ponder the relevance of their being philosophy majors.) In Steve's argument, one dissimilarity between the HD-DVD/Blu-Ray competition and the Betamax/VHS and 8-track/compact cassette competition is that the latter two involved size differences between the two formats (Betamax were smaller than VHS; 8-track tapes were larger than compact cassettes), and the former does not. Is this similarity relevant to whether one format will make the other obsolete? Ultimately, it depends on whether the sameness of size of HD-DVD and Blu-Ray discs somehow makes it less likely to render one or the other obsolete (which is not entirely clear). Fourth, stronger analogical arguments have *more diverse analogs*. Hence, if Andrew and Audra are from different ethnic backgrounds, that increases the strength of the argument. And fifth, stronger analogical arguments have *more modest conclusions*. Inferring that Susan likes ballroom dancing somewhat is stronger than the inference that she absolutely loves it. These five factors may be summarized as follows:

Principle for Evaluating Analogical Arguments
An analogical argument is strong the extent to which:
a. The number of analogs is greater.
b. The number of similarities between the subject and analogs is greater, and the number of dissimilarities between the subject and analogs is lower.
c. The relevance of the similarities between the subject and analogs is greater, and the relevance of the dissimilarities between the subject and analogs is lower.
d. The diversity of the analogs is greater.
e. The conclusion is more modest.

There are two approaches to measuring the degree of relevance of a similarity (or difference). For example, Audra and Susan's both being philosophy majors is less relevant to inferences about whether they like dancing than it would be for what classes they are taking. On one approach, it is a matter of whether having the similar property has an effect on the probability of the subject and analog's having the inferred property. On the other approach, relevance is understood as stemming from the similar property being the sort of thing that would be part of the explanation for why the subject and analogy might have that property. The relevance of a similarity or dissimilarity depends (in part) on the property that is being inferred in the subject.

Principle for Determining whether a Similarity or Dissimilarity Is Relevant in an Analogical Argument
Q is a relevant similarity or dissimilarity between w and x for the purpose of determining whether w has P if and only if
Q is a similarity or dissimilarity and either a w's or x's having (not having)
Q increases or decreases the probability of that w's or x's having (not having) P.
or

A w's or x's having (not having) Q is part of the explanation of why an w or x has (does not have) P.

9.1.1 A Logical Digression: Analogical Arguments versus Generalization and Particularization Arguments

One might wonder if it is possible to characterize an analogical argument as a disguised generalization and particularization argument. Consider the following analogical argument:

1. Samantha is a white, female, and a swan.
2. Sally is female and a swan.
3. Thus, Sally is probably white.

Could this argument be characterized as a disguised generalization (between 1 and 2) and then a particularization (from 2 to 3)?

1. Samantha is white, female, and a swan.
1.5. Thus, most female swans are white.
2. Sally is a female and a swan.
3. Thus, Sally is probably white.

While it is certainly possible for someone to offer this latter argument, one does not do so automatically by offering the first one. The latter argument makes a claim (1.5) that ranges over unnamed female swans (i.e., that most are white). The former argument makes no such generalization. It relies only on the similarities between Sally and Samantha and does not assert or assume any claim over other female swans. In principle, it could turn out that there is something particular about Sally and Samantha that makes both of them white that does not apply to other female swans.

10

EVALUATING HYPOTHESES: INFERENCE TO BEST EXPLANATION

In recent decades, a further variety of inductive reasoning has emerged into prominence: explanatory inference (also known as "inference to best explanation"). As philosophers have put greater emphasis on reasoning methods that capture the actual thinking in core areas of inquiry (such as the natural sciences), it has become clear that generalization, particularization, and analogical arguments are not the complete story for inductive reasoning. For example, one major limitation of each of these forms of reasoning is that one can only infer in one's conclusion the existence of a property that is also affirmed in one's premises (i.e., inferring P in an overall population on the basis of P in a sample or P in a subject because of P in an analog). However, there are surely cases in which one rightly infers the existence of a new property that is not contained in one's premises. If that is so, then a further variety of reasoning must be possible. And one major option is inference to best explanation, which many take to be a major form of reasoning employed in the natural sciences. In explanatory inference, it is possible to rightly infer the existence of a property that is not contained in one's premises (so long as that property is sufficiently explanatory). Thus, explanatory inference does not have the same limitation as generalization, particularization, and analogical arguments.

In inference to best explanation, a hypothesis is offered as a proposed explanation of a phenomenon. The objective in evaluating a hypothesis is to determine whether the hypothesis is true. And, in an explanatory inference, a hypothesis is inferred to be true because it would be the best explanation of a set of observations (hence the name "inference to best explanation").

Form of Explanatory Inference
1. H (if true) would explain $O_1, O_2, O_3 \ldots$
2. Thus, there is some probability n that H is true and explains $O_1, O_2, O_3 \ldots$

Since it is always easy to come up with potential explanations of any set of observations, the strength of an explanatory inference is based on how well the hypothesis would explain the observations. The hypothesis supported by the strongest inference is usually called the "best explanation." There are six factors that determine this: *likelihood, explanatory power, simplicity, novelty, appropriate explanatory content,* and *modesty of the conclusion relative to the premises.*

10.1 LIKELIHOOD

The likelihood of a hypothesis is (arguably) the most important factor in determining how well it explains a phenomenon. Likelihood is a type of conditional probability. It is the probability of certain evidence or observations given a certain hypothesis, that is, $P(O|H)$. Ultimately, the purpose of inference to best explanation is to determine the probability of the hypothesis given the observational data, that is, $P(H|O)$.

For a hypothesis to have any likelihood, it must be *testable.* A hypothesis is testable by virtue of making predictions. A prediction is a statement of the form "If one engages in action *A*, then one will observe *O*." Suppose my car won't start. The hypothesis that my car battery is dead is testable. For one can infer from it that "If I connect my car's battery to a charger overnight *(A)*, then my car will start *(O)*." By contrast, the hypothesis that the intelligent but undetectable beings that live on Saturn want my car not to start is not testable. For if that hypothesis is true, there are no observations that anyone could make in regard to it regardless of what actions are taken. Ideally, an explanatory hypothesis should be testable. However, untestable hypotheses are not automatically false or beyond rational evaluation. Some of the techniques in this chapter can still be applied to them. They simply cannot be *tested.*

For example, a murder was committed. Consider the hypothesis is that Mike did it. If Mike did it, then we can predict that his roommate Al will not be able to provide an alibi for him. Hence, if Al then fails to provide an alibi, then the hypothesis has made a successful prediction, which increases its likelihood. Note that this is the fallacy of affirming the consequence. So, when an observation increases the likelihood of a hypothesis, it is does not guarantee that it is true. Instead, it contributes to the inference's degree of strength. And stronger explanatory inferences have *higher probabilities for their (true) predictions*. The higher the probability is that Al will not provide an alibi, the greater the likelihood of the hypothesis. Note that it is often not possible to provide a specific numerical probability. Instead, the probabilities are often rough estimates (very high, low, and so on) or comparative ("If A, then O" is more probable on H_1 than on H_2).

When a hypothesis predicts that something will be observed to occur and it does not, then the likelihood of that hypothesis is decreased by that observation. And if the hypothesis predicts that the observation would occur with probability 1, then observation *falsifies* the hypothesis. In such a case, the predictions are guaranteed (if the hypothesis is true). And so the argument turns out to be deductive (denying the consequent). For example, if a detective holds that Mike the murderer acted alone, then that implies that Fran was not accomplice in the crime. But if it turns out that Fran is an accomplice, then the original theory is shown to be false. Falsification is an ideal that is rarely achieved. In most cases (where the probability of the observation is less than 1), the observation will simply decrease a hypothesis's likelihood but not guarantee that it is false.

Principle for Evaluating Likelihood
For hypothesis H, *observations* O, *and actions* A *undertaken to make them, the likelihood of* H *is* P(If A, then O|H).

Now, strictly speaking, most hypotheses do not (by themselves) make predictions. For example, the hypothesis that Mike is the murderer does not (alone) allow us to infer that there is a certain probability that his roommate Al will not be able to provide an alibi for him. That inference is possible only when the hypothesis is combined with additional claims about Mike's relationship to his roommate and more general claims about the probability of people lying to protect roommates when accused of murder. These further claims are *auxiliary assumptions*. Because both the hypothesis and the auxiliary assumptions are necessary in order to generate the predictions, there is a sense in which it is their conjunction that is tested. This is not much of a problem if the hypothesis and its auxiliary assumptions are affirmed, but in falsification it creates a problem: Is it the hypothesis or an auxiliary assumption that should be rejected? In principle, one could reasonably respond either way. However, ideally, one's auxiliary assumptions should already be well confirmed prior to being used in generating predictions of a hypothesis. In cases like that, the background information would make it more reasonable to reject the hypothesis than the auxiliary assumptions. However, if this cannot be done, then the hypothesis and the relevant auxiliary assumptions would have to be separated and further tests undertaken to determine which is reasonably rejected.

10.2 EXPLANATORY POWER

Stronger explanatory inferences have greater *explanatory power*. Something's explanatory power is based on the number of things that it explains. This is sometimes stated as a comparative matter between two hypotheses. One will have greater explanatory power if it explains everything the other does but also explains further things that the other does not. Sometimes this explanatory virtue is also referred to as "theoretical unity" or "unification potential." For example, Einstein's theory of relativity has greater explanatory power than Newton's laws of motion because while both explain the motions of bodies at "everyday" speeds, the theory of relativity also explains their motions as they get closer to the speed of light.

10.3 SIMPLICITY

Stronger explanatory inferences have greater *simplicity*. Something is simple based on the number of entities, properties, relations, or laws that it postulates (or the number of kinds of these things that it postulates). Alternatively, something can be simple based on the number of terms involved in a mathematical equation required to describe it.

Principles for Evaluating Simplicity
Hypothesis H is simpler than H* to the extent to which:
1. H postulates fewer entities, properties, relations, or laws.
2. H postulates fewer categories of entities, properties, relations, or laws.
3. H postulates fewer terms in any mathematical equation.

Consider the theory that there are undetectable gremlins that live in our shoes. That theory is less simple than the theory that there are no such undetectable gremlins. And since, by definition, there is no way to test either theory (no way to determine likelihood), the greater simplicity of the denial of undetectable gremlins makes it (relative to the evidence we have) a better hypothesis. Thus, untestable hypotheses may still be evaluated in terms of their simplicity. Testable hypotheses are also evaluated in terms of simplicity. For example, if someone discovers footprints in a forest and postulates that one elephant made them, that theory is simpler than the theory that the footprint was made by two elephants. The theory is also simpler than the hypothesis that the footprints were made by an elephant and a rhino. In both cases, one theory affirms a single entity, and the other affirms two. In addition, the theory that two elephants made the footprints is simpler than the theory that they were made by a rhino and elephant. Here, the number of entities is the same (two), but the number of kinds of entities differs. One theory only affirms elephants, and the other affirms elephants and rhinos. It is important to note that simplicity is always one of many factors used to assess explanations. So, the fact that one theory is simpler than the other does not automatically mean it is a better explanation if the other theory makes more true predictions. Simplicity typically factors in when two hypotheses are equally successful in their predictions but one does so with fewer entities.

10.4 NOVELTY

Stronger explanatory inferences have greater *novelty* or fruitfulness. Some hold that a theory gains more support from explaining things that were not known to be true at the time the theory was formed. Instead, these things were inferred to exist (or discovered) by the use of the hypothesis itself. Not all philosophers regard this principle to be legitimate; however, it is important to be aware of it since there are many who employ it.

Principle for Evaluating Explanatory Novelty
H *has novelty to the extent to which it successfully predicts* $O_1, O_2, O_3 \ldots$, *but* H *was formed at a time at which* $O_1, O_2, O_3 \ldots$ *were not expected to be true.*

For example, Newton's laws of motion predict a path for the orbit of Uranus that turns out not to match the actual observed motions unless one postulates a further planet affecting that orbit (via gravity). And it was through calculations with Newton's laws that led to the original postulation of Neptune. To some, that gives Newton's theory special support because of its explanatory novelty. It leads us to expect a further planet that we had (at that time) no other reason to affirm.

10.5 APPROPRIATE EXPLANATORY CONTENT

Strong explanatory inferences have *appropriate explanatory content*. For example, in the natural sciences, explanations can appeal only to physical/ natural entities. As such, nonphysical beings like God, souls, or Platonic Forms cannot be a part of a scientific explanation. However, in other contexts (such as philosophy), no such restriction exists. Nonphysical beings still face a major challenge to being part of the best explanatory theory. For they will have to overcome the fact that they are almost always less simple than their purely physical rivals and will have to make predictions about observable things despite the fact that they are not themselves observable (or perhaps rely on a theory of observation that goes beyond sensory and introspective experiences to include something like moral or conceptual "experiences"). Unlike the other factors, appropriate explanatory content is not a matter of degree. Either the content is suitable for the context or it is not.

10.6 SUMMARY OF FACTORS IN EVALUATING EXPLANATORY INFERENCES

In addition to likelihood, explanatory power, simplicity, novelty, and appropriate explanatory content, we must add modesty. Stronger explanatory inferences have more modest conclusions. Claiming that it is probable that Mike is the murderer makes for a stronger inference than claiming that it is very probable that he is the murderer. These factors may be summarized as follows.

Principle for Evaluating an Explanatory Inference
An explanatory inference of hypothesis H *is strong to the extent to which:*
a. H *has a higher likelihood.*
b. H *has greater explanatory power.*
c. H *is simpler.*
d. H *has greater novelty.*
e. H *has appropriate explanatory content.*
f. The conclusion is more modest (the probability n is lower).

The hypothesis that is supported by the strongest explanatory inferences is the *best explanation*.

10.7 EXPLANATORY INFERENCES, CONFIRMATION, DISCONFIRMATION, AND BAYES'S THEOREM

An alternate way to structure explanatory inferences is in terms of Bayes's theorem:

$$P(H|O) = \frac{P(O|H) \times P(H)}{P(O)}$$

According to Bayes's theorem, the probability of a hypothesis given certain facts (*H*'s *posterior probability*) is determined by multiplying the probability that it gives to that evidence (*H*'s *likelihood*) times the probability of the hypothesis independent of that evidence (*H*'s *prior probability*) all divided by the probability of that evidence (*O*'s *prior probability*). In such inferences, the likelihood of *H* is determined in the same way that it is in other explanatory inferences. However, to determine the final probability of *H* given *O*, one also has to know the prior probabilities of *H* and *O*.

The prior probability of *H* (its probability independent of *O*) is a complex issue. Sometimes it is nothing more than the probability of *H* given other evidence (i.e., given everything we knew before we found *O*). However, that itself is determined only by means of Bayes's theorem, and so the probability of *H* is independent of that evidence. Thus, there is the need to know the probability of *H* given no particular (contingent) facts. One way to assign this probability is in terms of some of the features involved in general explanatory inferences such as *H*'s *simplicity*. Therefore, if $P(O|H_1)$ = $P(O|H_2)$ but H_1 is simpler than H_2, then $P(H_1) > P(H_2)$, and so (by Bayes's theorem) $P(H_1|O) > P(H_2|O)$.

Another (very controversial) option for determining prior probabilities is the *principle of indifference*. This holds that all possibilities are equally probable unless there is reason to think otherwise (such as one having a greater simplicity). Where *A* is the ratio of favorable outcomes (*f*) to the number of possible outcomes (*n*), the following formula states the probability of *A*:

$$P(A) = \frac{f}{n}$$

So the probability that a coin toss will yield heads is $\frac{1}{2}$. The probability that the toss of a die will come up with a three (or any other possible outcome) is 1/6. The probability that one will draw a queen of hearts from a standard fifty-two-card poker deck is 1/52. The probability of drawing a king from a standard poker deck is 4/52 = 1/13 = 0.076923.

To use Bayes's theorem in explanatory inference, one simply plugs in the values for the likelihood of H and prior probabilities of H and O. The hypothesis that has the higher probability given all the relevant O's will be taken to be the *best explanation*.

Sometimes the extent of support that an observation provides to a hypothesis is put in terms of it *confirming* or *disconfirming* that hypothesis. Roughly, an observation confirms a hypothesis when its probability is greater given that observation than without it. And an observation disconfirms a hypothesis when its probability is lower given that observation than without it. (If its probability becomes 0, then that observation falsifies the hypothesis.) And an observation that neither increases nor decreases the probability of a hypothesis is confirmationally irrelevant to it.

Principle of Confirmation
O confirms H if and only if: P(H|O) > P(H)

Principle of Disconfirmation
O disconfirms H if and only if: P(H|O) < P(H)

Principle of Falsification
O falsifies H if and only if: P(H|O) = 0

Principle of Confirmational Irrelevance
O is confirmationally irrelevant to H if and only if: P(H|O) = P(H)

Some find usefulness in Bayes's theorem even though they are skeptical of assigning prior probabilities based on factors like simplicity. Instead, they use the likelihood of a hypothesis to make comparative judgments between hypotheses. For example, if two hypotheses predict that the same event will occur, and it does, but the first hypothesis gave that event a higher probability, then that event better confirms the first hypothesis. This strategy is known as the "likelihood principle."

Likelihood Principle
For some O, if the probability of O on H_1 is greater than the probability of O on H_2, then O is better supported by (or, is better explained by) H_1 than H_2.

Suppose that Wendy finds that one of husband Hal's shirts has lipstick on the collar that is not a color she uses. She hypothesizes that it got there because Hal is having an affair with another woman. But, Hal claims the lipstick got there because he was trying to find a new lipstick color to buy her as a present, and he put it up to his face to see how it matched his skin tone (since he and Wendy have similar skin tones) but got it on his collar by accident. The likelihood principle asks us to consider how probable each of these hypotheses make the lipstick on the collar. That is, if Hal were having an affair, what is the probability there would be lipstick on his collar? And if Hal were shopping for a new lipstick for Wendy, what is the probability that there would be lipstick on his collar? The hypothesis that confers a higher probability on the lipstick on the collar is the one that is better confirmed. And it would seem that things look bad for Hal (given only this evidence). Now, obviously, other evidence could change the outcome (such as if Hal has a receipt and gift-wrapped lipstick of this type in his desk drawer). This rule does not permit one to make a final assessment of the probability or truth of a hypothesis but makes a comparative judgment of which hypothesis is better confirmed by a particular set of facts. And in some contexts, that is sufficient.

NOTE

1. Sometimes an observation will be said to confirm a hypothesis if the hypothesis successfully predicts it. However, this can be very misleading. It is true that if H successfully predicts O, then $P(H|O) > P(H)$, assuming that $0 < \Pr(H) < 1$ and $\Pr(O) > 0$. However, one cannot assign $P(H|O)$ simply on the basis of how probable O is, given H. That would be to assume that $P(H|O) = P(O|H)$, which is, given Bayes's theorem, false. One *must* know (or at least estimate) $P(H)$ and $P(O)$ in order to determine $P(H|O)$.

CAUSAL INFERENCES

In a causal inference, one attempts to establish which event (or factor) brought about another event (or factor). There are different types of causes. Suppose that Matt lights a match. First, there is the *triggering* or *proximate* cause. This might be the match's striking against a rock. Second, there are the *structuring* causes. Structuring causes are the factors that create a tendency for the occurrence of one event to result in another. In the case of fire, the presence of oxygen is a structuring cause. Oxygen alone does not cause fire, but without oxygen, fire is not possible. Third, there are *distal* or *indirect* causes. These events bring about the triggering (or structuring) cause. In this case, it might be Matt's desire to start a fire for heat. Finally, there are *contributing* causes. These are further events that help to bring about one of the other sorts of causes but (for whatever reason) are less significant. So, while Matt may have lit the match primarily to start a fire for heat, he might also have a small tendency for pyromania that contributed somewhat to his lighting the match but not nearly as much as his desire for heat.

11.1 MILL'S METHODS OF CAUSAL INFERENCE

The nineteenth-century philosopher John Stuart Mill described five strategies for inferring causation. These methods can be conceived of as premises that permit one (with corresponding premises of the right content) to deduce that one event is probably the cause of another. As such, causal inferences are not so much a different *form* of reasoning as a set of *additional rules* or *types of premises* that can be used in particular contexts.

Suppose that two neighbors each buy a banana plant of the same size and age. Each one takes it home, and one gives it twice the recommended amount of water, and the other gives it twice the recommended amount of sunlight. However, both use three times the normal recommended amount of fertilizer. The next week, both plants have died. Since the only thing they both did was give their plants three times the normal amount of fertilizer, they infer that it killed their plants. This reasoning employs the *method of agreement*.

Method of Agreement

If the only similarity (agreement) in the (recent) history of two P-type events is the occurrence of Q-type events, then there is reason to believe that the Q-type events are the cause of the P-type events.

It is important to note that in all types of causal inference, the inference principle provides only "reason to believe" that one event causes another. These principles provide added tools in causal reasoning, but they do not provide certainty.

Now, one neighbor purchases two more banana plants of the same size and age. He provides both of them with the same (recommended) amount of water and light. But he provides one with the recommended dose of fertilizer and the other with three times the normal amount. The one that receives three times the normal amount dies in a week, and the other one is perfectly healthy. He notes that the history of the two plants is the same except for one factor: the amount of fertilizer. Thus, he infers that the additional fertilizer killed the second plant. This reasoning employs the *method of difference*.

Method of Difference

If the only dissimilarity (difference) in the (recent) history of the occurrence and nonoccurrence of a P-type event is the occurrence of a Q-type event prior to the P-type event, then there is reason to believe that the Q-type event is the cause of the P-type event.

It is possible to combine the two methods for added support. Let one of the neighbors buy three more new banana plants of the same size and age. He gives the first normal light, normal water, and twice as much fertilizer as recommended. He gives the second twice as much light, normal water, and twice as much fertilizer as recommended. He gives the third one normal light, normal water, and normal fertilizer. Then the two plants with twice as much fertilizer die in two weeks. He recognizes that the only thing common between the two that died and different between one of the ones that died and the one that lived is the double portion of fertilizer. Thus, he infers that the extra fertilizer killed the two banana plants. And the underlying principle is the *joint method of agreement and difference*.

Joint Method of Agreement and Difference
If the only similarity (agreement) in the (recent) history of two P-type events is the prior occurrence of Q-type event and the only dissimilarity (difference) in the (recent) history of the occurrence and nonoccurrence of a P-type event is the occurrence of a Q-type event prior to the P-type event, then there is reason to believe that the Q-type event is the cause of the P-type event.

Not to be outdone, the other neighbor goes out and buys six banana plants of the same size and age. He gives all of them the normal light, water, and fertilizer. But after a few weeks, he begins to give them (week by week) slowly more and more fertilizer (1.1 times normal, 1.2 times normal, and so forth up to 1.5 times normal as a maximum). The plants grow faster and faster as he gives them more and more fertilizer. He then recognizes that the increase in fertilizer (up to 1.5 times normal) also increased with the plant growth rate. The two varied together. He then infers that the fertilizer was a cause of the added growth. This reasoning employs the *method of concomitant variation*.

Method of Concomitant Variation
If the prior increase or decrease of Q-type events in a population increases or decreases prior the occurrence of P-type events in that population, then there is reason to believe that the Q-type events are the cause(s) of the P-type events.

This method may also be employed to infer causation with the decrease of a property. Perhaps the decrease of water in the banana plants also varies with a decrease in their health. In addition, causation may be inferred when an increase varies with a decrease or when a decrease varies with an increase. Perhaps the increase of fertilizer over 1.5 times the recommended amount varies with a decrease in health, or a decrease in fertilizer from 2.0 times the recommended amount varies with an increase in their health.

One neighbor increased the amount of fertilizer by half and increased the amount of water given to his banana plants by a third. The yield increased. He knew that part of the increased yield could be attributed to the fertilizer. He concluded that the remainder of the increase was caused by the increase in water. This method employs the *method of residues*.

Method of Residues
If there are two complex phenomena and some elements of one are known to be causally correlated with elements of the other, it is likely that the remaining elements are also causally correlated.

11.2 PROBABILISTIC METHOD OF CAUSAL INFERENCE

Mill's methods are not the only approaches to causal inference. There are other strategies based on particular theories of the nature of causation. Naturally, these methods tend to be favored by those who also adopt the underlying theory of causation.

The first approach takes causation to consist in one event's increasing or decreasing the probability of another. For example, if someone who has a cold sits next to me for three hours constantly coughing, that might increase the probability of my contracting a cold. Thus, if I end up getting a cold, there would be reason to regard my exposure to that person as *positively causally relevant* to (a *positive cause* of) my cold. If my friend also sat next to the person who had the cold but she has a diet that is much richer in vitamin C, that might decrease her probability of getting a cold. If she does not get a cold, then there would be reason to regard her high level of vitamin C as *negatively causally relevant* to (a *preventative cause* of) her getting a cold. If another friend did not get exposed to the person who was sick but instead spent the day sitting in the rain yet gets a cold anyway, they might think that their sitting in the rain caused them to get a cold. However, if it turns out that sitting in the rain does not increase or decrease the probability of getting a cold, then the sitting in the rain is *causally irrelevant* to (not a cause of) their getting a cold. These inferences employ the following principles.

Probabilistic Model of Causation Inference Principles
If E_1 occurs prior to E_2 and $P(E_2|E_1) > P(E_2|not\text{-}E_1)$, then there is reason to believe that E_1 is positively causally relevant to E_2 (a positive cause).

If E_1 *occurs prior to* E_2 *and* $P(E_2|E_1) < P(E_2|\text{not-}E_1)$, *then there is reason to believe that* E_1 *is negatively causally relevant to* E_2 *(a preventative cause).*

If E_1 *occurs prior to* E_2 *and* $P(E_2|E_1) = P(E_2|\text{not-}E_1)$, *then there is reason to believe that* E_1 *is causally irrelevant to* E_2 *(not a cause).*

11.3 COUNTERFACTUAL METHOD OF CAUSAL INFERENCE

Beyond the probabilistic method, one may also employ counterfactuals to support causal claims. A *counterfactual* is a conditional statement about what would (or might) occur in a particular alternate scenario such as "If the second baseman hadn't dropped the ball, then his team would have won the game." Establishing that statements of this type are true can be a complex task and is discussed in the next chapter. However, once one has established counterfactual claims, one can often use them to infer causation.

On a counterfactual theory of causation, causally related events are such that each one has a prior one (somewhere in the sequence) without which it would not have occurred; that is, the counterfactual "If event E_1 had not occurred, then event E_2 would not have occurred" is true. Those who endorse this view of causation can employ the *counterfactual method of causal inference.*

Counterfactual Model of Causation Inference Principle
If E_1 *occurs prior to* E_2, *and if* E_1 *had not occurred, then* E_2 *would not have occurred, then there is reason to believe that* E_1 *is a cause of* E_2.

If a second baseman drops a fly ball in the ninth inning with two outs and runners on second and third who score to win the game, then it is (plausibly) true that if he hadn't dropped it, his team would have won the game. As such, one could infer that his dropping the ball is one of the causes of his team's losing the game.

COUNTERFACTUAL REASONING

Statements about what would (or might) occur in a particular alternate scenario are called "counterfactuals." For example, the statement "If Vanessa had not missed her free throws with 10 seconds left in a tied game, then her team would have won the game" is a counterfactual. These statements are often used to support causal claims (see section 11.3 in chapter 11) or to retrospectively analyze a situation. Vanessa's team might appeal to the above counterfactual in support of the idea that their poor free-throw shooting cost them the game.

12.1 SUPPORTING COUNTERFACTUAL CLAIMS

Supporting a counterfactual claim is a complex task. It can be divided into three parts. First, one has to select the *antecedent scenario*. There are usually many possible ways that the counterfactual's antecedent could have been true. For example, Vanessa might not have missed her free throws by (1) making them both; (2) missing the first but making the second; (3) making the first, missing the second, and her team gets the rebound; (4) making the first, missing the second, and her team does not get the rebound; and so forth. Second, one has to develop the scenario by selecting the *intermediate states*. Many events occur between the time of the antecedent scenario and the time of the counterfactual's consequent. For example, the opposing team calls a time-out, runs a pick-and-roll off the inbound pass, takes a final shot, and misses. Each of these actually occurred after Vanessa missed her two free throws. But whether they also would have occurred if she had not missed them both is important to determining the truth of the counterfactual. And third, one has to select the *scenario outcome*. Every counterfactual projects something for a particular period of time; what happens at that time is the scenario outcome (such as Vanessa's team winning or not winning the game).

Since there are three parts to establishing a counterfactual claim, there are three factors involved in whether a counterfactual is reasonable to accept.

Principle for Supporting a Counterfactual
The counterfactual "if it were the case that p, then it would be the case that q"
is reasonable to accept as true *the extent to which:*
a. The antecedent scenario for p is *plausible.*
b. The intermediate states between the time of p and the time of q are *not undermined by the antecedent scenario.*
c. The outcome scenario that includes q is *probable (given the antecedent scenario and intermediate states).*

An *antecedent scenario* begins at the point one introduces a deviation (change) from what actually happened. The antecedent scenario ends at the point at which the antecedent of the counterfactual is true. Thus, the antecedent scenario is the "backstory" for the counterfactual. Antecedents and scenarios are assessed in terms of whether there are *highly* improbable events in the scenario (none is preferred), the length of the scenario (shorter is better), and the probability of the original deviation that begins the scenario (better to reverse an improbable event than to reverse a probable one).

Principle for Assessing an Antecedent Scenario's Plausibility
An antecedent scenario is plausible *the extent to which:*
a. It does not include any highly improbable events.
b. The series of events (deviating from what actually happened) that leads to the antecedent is shorter.
c. The original deviation reverses an improbable event rather than a probable one.

These factors interact with each other, and one may have to trade off between them. Ultimately, they are listed in an order of priority. For example, if Vanessa is an absolutely terrible free-throw shooter, then one would have to have a longer scenario in order to go back and increase her free-throw percentage (perhaps by practicing at halftime, or before the game, or for weeks before). But if she could be said to make shots without it being too highly improbable, then that would be the place to intervene. (Shorter scenarios are better unless they require highly improbable events.) Now, the shortest scenario would be one where she makes only the second free throw (for the scenario would deviate from history after she misses the first). However, that sort of shortness is not always significant. There might be reason to choose the longer scenario where she makes the first one if, for example, she is always much better at her first free throw than her second. In that case, the scenario is more plausible if she makes the first one (since it reverses an improbable event rather than a probable one). Now, if she makes the first one in the antecedent scenario, then the antecedent is true, and so whether she makes the second is a matter of intermediate states.

The intermediate states are those events that occur between the time of the antecedent scenario becoming true and the time of the consequent in the counterfactual. These events come from two sources: (1) events that actually happened in that time and (2) events that are part of supporting counterfactuals with the same antecedent as the one in question.

Principle for Assessing an Intermediate State's Being Undermined
An intermediate state is not undermined by the antecedent scenario the extent to which (one of the following):
a. It actually occurred and its probability is unaffected by the antecedent scenario (and any prior intermediate states), or
b. It actually occurred and its probability is only increased by the antecedent scenario (and any prior intermediate states), or
c. It is the consequent of a true supporting counterfactual with the same antecedent as the one under consideration.[1]

The opposing team called a time-out after Vanessa missed. Suppose that their coach is just as likely to do so regardless of whether she makes or misses them (this is his standard policy). In that case, the calling of time out is not undermined by the antecedent scenario (Vanessa not missing the free throws) because its probability is unaffected by it. The opposing team also ran a pick-and-roll to take a final shot. Now, since the antecedent scenario puts them in a different position of being down (instead of tied) with ten seconds left, there is some effect on the probability of their choice of a final play. But suppose that they are only more likely to run a pick-and-roll in such cases. Then that event is also not undermined by the antecedent scenario.

The most controversial (and critical) intermediate states are whether Vanessa makes her second free throw and whether the other team misses their last shot. Ultimately, the opposing team's being down (instead of tied) would seem to affect the probability of their missing the last shot (and not simply by increasing that probability). So, whether they make or miss that last shot is something that has to be assessed as a supporting counterfactual. That is, one considers whether that would be part of a probable outcome scenario (if this were the place the counterfactual ended). The same seems true of Vanessa's missing her second free throw. (If one cannot reasonably support a counterfactual concluding that she makes it or one that she does not, then one cannot include either event. The scenario must remain neutral.)

The scenario outcome is a fairly straightforward matter to discover. Once one has determined the antecedent scenario and intermediate states, one simply considers all the possible outcomes consistent with them. To the extent to which they include the outcome scenario, that outcome scenario is probable (i.e., percentage of cases where it holds).

Principle for Assessing an Outcome Scenario Probability
An outcome scenario is probable *the extent to which all the possible scenarios that are consistent with the antecedent scenario and intermediate states contain the elements of the outcome scenario.*

Some prefer to claim only that a particular outcome *would* occur if it holds in all possible scenarios (consistent with the antecedent scenario and intermediate states) and that a particular outcome *might* occur if it holds in at least one of them. Others simply let the consequent be a statement about the probability that a particular outcome would occur. And still others are willing to say that an outcome would occur if it is the most probable of the options.

12.1.1 A Logical Digression: Counterfactual Fallacies

Counterfactual conditionals cannot be treated as if they were standard conditionals. As such, there are a number of inferences that one can make with standard conditionals that one cannot make with counterfactuals. They include:

Counterfactual Hypothetical Syllogism
1. If it were the case that p, *then it would be the case that* q.
2. If it were the case that q, *then it would be the case that* r.
3. So, if it were the case that p, *then it would be the case that* r.

The reason that this need not hold for counterfactuals is that the changes one may introduce to get p, and then q (in 1), may be different from those one has to introduce to get only q, and then r (in 2). And, since it is the changes one introduces to get p that matter for 3, they will not necessarily have to include r.

Counterfactual Disjunctive Syllogism
1. Either q or not-q.
2. It is false that: If it were the case that p, then it would be the case that q.
3. So, if it were the case that p, then it would be the case that not-q.

The reason this does not hold is that q and not-q might be equally probable given the antecedent scenario for p and the intermediate states between p and q.

NOTE

1. For a sophisticated formal discussion of this issue, see Igal Kvart, *A Theory of Counterfactual* (Indianapolis: Hackett, 1986).

⓭

DECISIONS UNDER RISK

Life is full of decisions. When the decisions concern something especially important to us, they frequently involve stress. For example, Dale is torn about whether to accept a lucrative job offer from a major law firm in New York or to stay in her small town so she can be close to her boyfriend. The anxiety from a decision frequently stems from there being multiple possible consequences (some good and some bad) that depend on which decision is made where there is no certainty as to which would obtain given each decision. In Dale's case, if she goes to New York, her career may flourish, but her relationship with her boyfriend could collapse, and if she stays, her relationship might flourish, but she might never get another chance to work at a major law firm. In such cases, we are often regulated to guessing or simply hoping about what is the best option. However, there is another alternative. "Rational decision theory" is the study of decision making and is essential to a full picture of critical thinking. Since the difficulty in decision making is often because we do not know (with certainty) what will be the consequences of our decisions, decision theory focuses on this. If we know the probability of each of the possible consequences, then we are making a decision under *risk*. But if we do not know the probabilities of the potential consequences but only what the possible consequences are, then that is decision making under *uncertainty* (which is the subject of the next chapter).

13.1 UTILITY

A decision's utility is the extent to which the agent making the decision re-
gards it (and its consequences) to be desirable or valuable. This can be as
simple as the amount of pleasure or happiness they produce, or the extent
to which they achieve particular goals, or how well they fit with the agent's
moral or political beliefs. Thus, the concept of "utility" is meant to be con-
strued broadly (not merely in terms of, say, the pleasure the agent receives):

Principle for Determining Utility
A D_1's consequence C_1 has utility U_1 to the extent to which it is desirable, goal-
fulfilling, and/or value conforming and so forth for the agent making the deci-
sion.

In some contexts, for example, economic ones, there is a specific preex-
isting number that can be used to define utility. In other contexts, one has
to assign a value. This is usually done on a scale from 0 to 100. It is often
stipulated that, for purposes of the decision in question, at least one of the
possible consequences will have a value of 100. In addition, more than one
consequence may have the same utility.

13.2 DECISION MAKING UNDER RISK WITH ONE FACTOR

Suppose that I prefer well-made chili to a well-made hamburger, but I prefer a not-well-made hamburger to not-well-made chili. If I must choose between chili and a hamburger but do not know if they are going to be well
made, then my decision should be based on which one has the highest *expected utility*.

Decision Making under Risk Principle
If the consequences $(C_1, C_2, C_3 \ldots)$ of possible decisions $(D_1, D_2, D_3 \ldots)$ are
not known with certainty but can be assigned probabilities, then the most rea-
sonable decision is the one whose consequences have the highest expected
utility.

Determining expected utility involves both the utility of the consequences and their probability. For example, suppose that the utility of well-
made chili is 100, a well-made hamburger is 80, a not-well-made hamburger is 60, and not well-made chili is 40. Now suppose that the

probability of getting a well-made hamburger (if ordered) is 0.75 (75 percent) and that the probability of getting well-made chili (if ordered) is 0.50
(50 percent). The expected utility of ordering a hamburger will be the utility of it well made (80) times the probability of it well made (0.75) plus its
utility not well made (60) times its probability not well made (0.25). (Note
that the probability here of all possible consequences added together must
be 1.00.) Doing the calculations, $(80 \times 0.75) + (60 \times 0.25) = 75$. In a similar way, the expected utility of ordering chili will be the utility of it well
made (100) times the probability of it well made (0.50) plus its utility not
well made (40) times its probability not well made (0.50). Doing these calculations, $(100 \times 0.50) + (40 \times 0.50) = 70$. Therefore, the expected utility
of the hamburger is 75, and the expected utility of the chili is 70. The reasonable decision to make is the hamburger.

Principle for Determining Expected Utility
The expected utility of decision D's consequences (when D has possible con-
sequences C_1, C_2, C_3 . . . that occur with probability P_1, P_2, P_3 . . . and have
utilities U_1, U_2, U_3 . . .) is $(U_1 \times P_1) + (U_2 \times P_2) + (U_3 \times P_3)$ . . .

Sometimes decision problems under risk are represented in terms of a
matrix that displays the possible decisions (rows) against the possible consequences (columns) with utilities and probabilities at their intersections.

	C1: Well-Made	C2: Not Well-Made	Expected Utility
D1: Hamburger	U = 80, P = 0.75	U = 60, P = 0.25	80 × 0.75 + 60 × 0.25 = 75
D2: Chili	U = 100, P = 0.50	U = 40, P = 0.50	100 × 0.50 + 40 × 0.50 = 70

13.3 DECISION MAKING UNDER RISK
WITH MULTIPLE FACTORS

In decision making under risk, one can assign utilities in two different ways.
First, one can assign them "all things considered." This is what was done in
the hamburger/chili case. The utilities reflect the sum total of my prefer-
ences on the matter including both taste and price. Second, in some contexts, it may be useful to break things down further in terms of different
possible factors. Suppose I choose my dessert on this basis. I might begin
by assigning utilities given *taste alone*. The setup and calculations might be:

Factor: Taste	C1: Well-Made	C2: Not Well-Made	Expected Utility
D1: Milkshake	U = 80, P = 0.80	U = 40, P = 0.20	80 × 0.80 + 40 × 0.20 = 72
D2: Sundae	U = 100, P = 0.60	U = 60, P = 0.40	100 × 0.60 + 60 × 0.40 = 84

Now I assign utilities given *price alone*; the setup and calculations might be:

Factor: Taste	C1: Well-Made	C2: Not Well-Made	Expected Utility
D1: Milkshake	U = 100, P = 0.80	U = 80, P = 0.20	100 × 0.80 + 80 × 0.20 = 96
D2: Sundae	U = 80, P = 0.60	U = 20, P = 0.40	80 × 0.60 + 20 × 0.40 = 56

So, determining the expected utility of a decision for a given factor runs as follows:

Principle for Determining Expected Utility for a Given Factor
The expected utility of decision D's consequences given factor F_1 (when D has possible consequences C_1, C_2, C_3 ... that occur with probability P_1, P_2, P_3 ... and have utilities U_1, U_2, U_3 ... given F_1) is ((U_1 given F_1) × P_1) + ((U_2 given F_1) × P_2) + ((U_3 given F_1) × P_3) ...

To determine the expected utility of a decision's consequences given all factors requires that we take into account the expected utilities of each decision for each factor as well as the importance that the agent attaches to each factor. This is the *relative weight* of a factor. Each factor has a percentage (out of 100) that represents its importance. (The total of relative weights of all factors must be 100 percent.) In this case, I might assign price the relative weight of 40 percent and taste a relative weight of 60 percent. I can then form an "all things considered" matrix. That places the factors along the columns instead of the possible consequences. And, in the intersecting points, it includes the expected utility and relative weight. For this example, it would look as follows:

Factor: All	F1: Taste	F2: Price	Expected Utility
D1: Milkshake	EU = 72, RW = 0.60	EU = 96, RW = 0.40	72 × 0.60 + 96 × 0.40 = 81.6
D2: Sundae	EU = 84, RW = 0.60	EU = 56, RW = 0.40	84 × 0.60 + 56 × 0.40 = 72.8

In the final calculation, the milkshake comes out with the highest expected utility. Determining expected utility for multiple-factors run can be described as:

Principle for Determining Expected Utility for All Factors
The expected utility of decision D's consequences given all factors (where D has expected utility EU_1 given factor F_1, EU_2 given factor F_2, and EU_3 given factor F_3, and F_1 has relative weight RW_1, F_2 has relative weight RW_2, and F_3 has relative weight RW_3 ...) is (EU_1 × RW_1) + (EU_2 × RW_2) + (EU_3 × RW_3) ...

Returning to Dale's decision about whether to accept the lucrative offer in New York or to stay in the small town, there seem to be two different factors to consider: her career and her relationship with her boyfriend. In the first case, there are two major consequences: her career flourishes or flounders (one may also introduce varying degrees of each of these). In the second case, there are two major consequences: her relationship flourishes or flounders (also admitting of degrees). Here are two potential matrices that she might form:

Factor: Career	C1: Flourish	C2: Flounder	Expected Utility
D1: Go to NY	U = 80, P = 0.90	U = 0, P = 0.10	80 × 0.90 + 0 × 0.10 = 72
D2: Stay Here	U = 100, P = 0.20	U = 20, P = 0.80	100 × 0.20 + 20 × 0.80 = 36

Factor: Relationship	C1: Flourish	C2: Flounder	Expected Utility
D1: Go to NY	U = 100, P = 0.05	U = 20, P = 0.95	100 × 0.05 + 20 × 0.95 = 24
D2: Stay Here	U = 80, P = 0.70	U = 0, P = 0.30	80 × 0.70 + 0 × 0.30 = 56

Now suppose she assigns a relative weight of 0.30 to her relationship and 0.70 to her career; the combined matrix would be:

Factor: All	F1: Career	F2: Relationship	Expected Utility
D1: Go to NY	EU = 72, RW = 0.70	EU = 24, RW = 0.30	72 × 0.70 + 24 × 0.30 = 57.6
D2: Stay Here	EU = 36, RW = 0.70	EU = 56, RW = 0.30	36 × 0.70 + 56 × 0.30 = 42

(14)

DECISIONS UNDER UNCERTAINTY

If we know the possible consequences of a decision but not their probability, then that decision is made under *uncertainty*. There are two types of decisions under uncertainty: *multilateral* and *unilateral*. If the consequences depend on another agent's decision, then the decision is multilateral (more than one agent is making a decision). If the consequences do not depend on another agent's decisions, then the decision is unilateral. Because of this difference, there are three types of principles for decision under uncertainty: (1) universal principles (for multilateral and unilateral decision making), (2) multilateral-only principles, and (3) unilateral-only principles. In addition, there is a priority among these principles. The order in which they are presented here reflects that sequence, that is, universal first, then either multilateral or unilateral, and in the same order as they appear in each section. In addition, the following principles do not cover all possibilities; these are simply the basic rules.

In decision making under uncertainty, since there is no knowledge of the probabilities of any potential consequences, utilities are often simplified to single-digit numbers. That is, instead of assigning them a value of 0 to 100, they are assigned in order of preference from highest to lowest (e.g., 5, 4, 3, 2, 1, and so on). Sometimes 0 and negative numbers are also used. Decisions are sometimes also called "strategies" and consequences "outcomes" (unilateral uncertainty) or "opposing strategies" (in multilateral uncertainty).

14.1 UNIVERSAL PRINCIPLES FOR
DECISIONS UNDER UNCERTAINTY

Suppose that I have to buy an expensive $100 book for a class, but I see it for $50 at a used bookstore. It is also possible that the used book is actually a first edition, in which case it is worth $500. I cannot determine the probability of its being an actual first edition, but it is possible. I have two options: buy used or buy new. Clearly, my order of preferences are (from lowest to highest) as follows: (1) buy new and used copy was a first edition, (2) buy new and used copy was not a first edition, (3) buy used and it was not a first edition, and (4) buy used and it was a first edition. If I represent these utilities on a matrix, they would be as follows:

	C1: Used Is First Edition	C2: Used Is Not First Edition
D1: Buy Used	4	3
D2: Buy New	1	2

If I buy the book used, my utilities will be higher regardless of whether it is a first edition or not (I get a 4 or 3 instead of a 1 or 2). While I do not know the probability of its being a first edition, I do know that I am still better off (in both cases) than if I buy the book new. The decision to buy used is said to *strongly dominate* the decision to buy new.

Principle for Determining Strong Dominance
D_1 *strongly dominates* D_2 *if and only if the possible outcomes of consequences* $C_1, C_2, C_3 \ldots$ *all have a higher utility on decision* D_1 *than on decision* D_2.

When one decision is strongly dominant over all other options, then there is reason to choose that option. In this case, there is reason to buy used rather than new.

Strong Dominance Principle for Decision Making under Uncertainty
If decision D_1 *strongly dominates all other possible decisions* $D_2, D_3 \ldots$, *then there is reason to choose* D_1.

Imagine that we add a further option to the above case in which I can borrow a copy of the book for free. This changes the utilities to something like the following:

	C1: Used Is First Edition	C2: Used Is Not First Edition
D1: Buy Used	6	4
D2: Buy New	1	3
D3: Borrow	2	5

In this case, buying used is no longer strongly dominant. The best option is still buying used if it is a first edition. But if it is not a first edition, I would have been better off borrowing the book. So, the strong dominance principle cannot be applied. However, even though buying used does not dominate all the other options, it does dominate buying new. There is a possible case where it is better not to buy used (if the used copy is not a first edition, then I should borrow the book). But there is *no* case where it is better to buy new (either I lose the chance to sell the used copy for $500 or I am simply out $100 for the new copy). Therefore, it is reasonable to eliminate the decision to buy new altogether. The principle that underlies this is as follows:

Strong Dominance Elimination Principle for Decision Making under Uncertainty
If decision D_1 is strongly dominated by at least one other possible decision D_2, then there is reason not to choose D_1.

In this case, borrowing also strongly dominates buying new, but it is not necessary to have more than one decision strongly dominate a decision to eliminate it. One is sufficient.

All decisions made under uncertainty are reasonably assessed first with these two principles. If these do not settle the matter, then one will proceed along somewhat different lines depending on whether it is a case of multilateral or unilateral uncertainty.

14.2 FURTHER PRINCIPLES FOR DECISIONS UNDER MULTILATERAL UNCERTAINTY

If the consequences of one's decision depend on the decision of another, then a new dynamic is introduced, namely, the other agent's utilities. This is significant because if you know their utilities, you may be able to project their decisions, which may affect what it is reasonable for you to do. And, of course, they may be able to do the same. Because of this back-and-forth thinking about what the other will/will not do, the study of decision making under multilateral uncertainty is called *game theory*, and the decision makers are called *players*. Strategic contexts that involve multiple decision makers are taken to be analogous to a "game." There are many different types of games, such as zero-sum games, in which any gain of utility for one player implies a loss for the other. And there are cooperative games where players have the chance to communicate and form enforceable agreements. Ultimately, these are subjects for another occasion. The most basic principles for decision making under multilateral uncertainty are as follows.

First, one can apply strong dominance. If you have a decision that strongly dominates all others available, then it is reasonable for you to use it. In that case, the other player's options do not really matter. In addition, if you have a decision that is strongly dominated by another possible decision, then it is reasonable for you to eliminate that possible decision. However, this introduces a new possibility not present in unilateral uncertainty: you may also eliminate consequences if one of them consists in a decision that is (for the other player) strongly dominated. For example, a small newspaper (player 1) and a large newspaper (player 2) decide how to respond to a major report on their declining readership. They can either do nothing (D_1/d_1), cut prices (D_2/d_2), or print a salacious exposé on the other (D_3/d_3). Suppose the utilities are as follows (with player 1's options D_1, D_2, D_3 along rows and player 2's options d_1, d_2, d_3 along the columns and the utilities represented as (player 1's, player 2's)):

	d1: Nothing	d2: Cut Price	d3: Exposé
D1: Nothing	(0, 2)	(0, 1)	(0, 2)
D2: Cut Price	(2, 0)	(1, 3)	(1, 3)
D3: Exposé	(4, 1)	(1, 1)	(5, 5)

Note that player 1's D_1 (nothing) is strongly dominated (by both D_2 and D_3). So, it can be eliminated, and the matrix becomes:

	d1: Nothing	d2: Cut Price	d3: Exposé
~~D1: Nothing~~	~~(0, 2)~~	~~(0, 1)~~	~~(0, 2)~~
D2: Cut Price	(2, 0)	(1, 3)	(1, 3)
D3: Exposé	(4, 1)	(1, 1)	(5, 5)

This opens up the possibility for a further elimination. Originally, player 2's d_2 (cut price) was not strongly dominated by their choice of d_3 (exposé), for both offered a utility of 2 if player 1 chose D_1 (nothing). Now that D_1 (nothing) is eliminated for player 1, player 2 faces utilities of 0 or 1 if they chose d_1 (nothing) versus 3 or 5 if they chose d_3 (exposé). Thus, player 2's d_1 (nothing) is strongly dominated now by d_3 (exposé) and can be eliminated. Now the matrix becomes:

	d1: Nothing	d2: Cut Price	d3: Exposé
D1: Nothing	(0, 2)	(0, 1)	(0, 2)
D2: Cut Price	(2, 0)	(1, 3)	(1, 3)
D3: Exposé	(4, 1)	(1, 1)	(5, 5)

Thus, the only options worth considering further for either player are D_2/d_2 (cutting price) and D_3/d_3 (printing an exposé). So, in multilateral uncertainty, considering the utilities of two players opens up the possibility for a cascading series of eliminations. The principle behind them is:

Strong Dominance–Iterated Elimination Principle for Multilateral Decision Making under Uncertainty
If one player has a decision D_1/d_1 that is strongly dominated by at least one of that player's other possible decisions D_2/d_2, then there is reason to reassess the options (for both players) without D_1/d_1.

When further iterations of strong dominance elimination fail to fully resolve a decision under multilateral uncertainty, one turns to what decision would be the *best reply* to a particular opposing decision. That is, one looks for the decision such that no other of that agent's decisions would yield a higher utility (for a particular opposing decision). Such decisions (there can be more than one) constitute a player's best reply. For example, player 1's best reply to player 2's printing an exposé would be also to print an exposé (it would give player 1 a payoff of 5 instead of 1). There can be more than one best reply. For example, player 2's best reply to player 1 cutting prices would be either cutting prices or printing an exposé (both have a utility of 3).

Principle for Determining Best Replies
D_1 is a player's best reply to the opposing player's d_1 if and only if D_1 has a utility that is no worse than D_2, or D_3 ... if the opposing player makes decision d_1.

In and of themselves, best replies are not especially useful. After all, neither player knows (at this point) what the other will do. However, when each of a pair of strategies (one for each player) is the best reply to the other, a new possibility emerges. Consider if both players print an exposé. In that case, each player has adopted the best reply to the other's decision. As such, neither player would have any reason (on their own) to change decisions (they would end up with a lower utility). Such pairs of best replies are a kind of equilibrium in the game (often called *Nash equilibria*). They provide a stable resolution of it (no one has reason to change). As such, there will be reason to adopt those strategies.

> *Best Reply (Nash) Equilibrium Principle for Multilateral Decision Making under Uncertainty*
> *If there are a pair of decisions (one for each player) D_1 and d_1 that are the best reply to each other and if there is no reason for the players not to want that combination of decisions, then each player has reason to choose D_1 and d_1.*

Here is where things begin to get very complex, for there can be more than one best reply (Nash) equilibrium. In this example, both players cutting prices is also one. Thus, there will need to be some further principle used to decide between the two. In this case, there might seem to be one: both players are better off if they adopt the exposé approach (player 1 gets 5 over 1, and player 2 gets 5 over 3). This is sometimes termed *Pareto optimal*. Unfortunately, cases with multiple equilibria do not always work out this way. And there are cases that do not have any equilibria (of this kind). So, once again, the principles laid out here are only very basic ones for decision under multilateral uncertainty. They will not solve all cases, but they will resolve some and make progress in many others.

14.3 FURTHER PRINCIPLES FOR DECISIONS UNDER UNILATERAL UNCERTAINTY

Because decisions under unilateral uncertainty involve a choice by only one agent, there is no need to assign utilities for more than one person. Others may be affected, but they are not making a decision. As such, the further principles for decision making under multilateral uncertainty do not apply. The universal principles apply, but since those are often not enough to resolve the problem, there are special principles for decision making under unilateral uncertainty that are worth mentioning. It is very important to note that one should *not* try to apply the following principles to cases of decision under multilateral uncertainty. These are formulated and ordered only for cases of unilateral uncertainty.

Suppose that my original choice of the new book or a used one that might be a first edition is modified a bit. Suppose that the price of the used copy is such that if it is not a first edition, then I am no better off than if I had bought the new one. In that case, the matrix would be:

	C1: Used Is First Edition	C2: Used Is Not First Edition
D1: Buy Used	2	1
D2: Buy New	1	1

Unlike the original example, buying the used copy is not strongly dominant. For while buying used yields a higher utility if the used one is a first edition (2 vs. 1), the utilities are equal if it is not a first edition. However, even though there is no guarantee of a higher utility, there is the possibility of one and a guarantee of no lower utility. In this case, buying used *weakly dominates* buying new.

Principle for Determining Weak Dominance
D_1 *weakly dominates* D_2 *if and only if at least one possible consequence* C_1 *has a higher utility on decision* D_1 *than on decision* D_2 *and the remaining consequences* $C_2, C_3 \ldots$ *have no worse a utility on decision* D_1 *than on* D_2.

Because buying used weakly dominates all other options, there is reason to choose the used copy.

Weak Dominance Principle for Unilateral Decision Making under Uncertainty
If decision D_1 *weakly dominates all other possible decisions* $D_2, D_3 \ldots$, *then there is reason to choose* D_1.

Even if there is no decision that weakly dominates all others, as with strong dominance, there may be one that is weakly dominated by another decision. Suppose we add on the possibility of borrowing the book to the modified example. And imagine that I am equally satisfied with borrowing if it is not a first edition as if I buy new and it is a first edition.

	C1: Used Is First Edition	C2: Used Is Not First Edition
D1: Buy Used	3	1
D2: Buy New	1	1
D3: Borrow	1	2

Now, buying used is no longer weakly dominant over all other decisions. (If the used book is not a first edition, there is a higher utility in borrowing one.) However, buying new is weakly dominated by buying used and borrowing. As such, there is reason not to buy new. That option can be eliminated.

> *Weak Dominance Elimination Principle for Unilateral Decision Making under Uncertainty*
>
> *If decision D_1 is weakly dominated by at least one other possible decision D_2, then there is reason not to choose D_1.*

When strong and weak dominance and elimination fail to resolve a case, there are two options worth considering. One is to select the decision that has the highest possible utility for its lowest utility. This is often termed the *maximin strategy*, as it involves securing the maximum for one's minimum possible payoff.

> *Maximin Principle for Unilateral Decision Making under Uncertainty*
>
> *If the lowest possible utility for D_1 is higher than the lowest possible utility for $D_2, D_3 \ldots$, then there is reason to choose D_1.*

In this example, neither decision is better via this approach since both have a minimum utility of 1. However, in the earlier version of this example, where buying used had utilities of 6 or 4 and borrowing had 2 or 5, this principle would make a difference. It would lead one to buy used. One guarantees at least a utility of 4.

The other option is to select the decision that has the highest utility for its highest possible utility. This is sometimes called the *maximax strategy*, as it involves securing the maximum possible maximum utility.

> *Maximax Principle for Unilateral Decision Making under Uncertainty*
>
> *If the highest possible utility for D_1 is higher than the highest possible utility for $D_2, D_3 \ldots$, then there is reason to choose D_1.*

In the above example, I might reasonably prefer to buy used because that has the highest possible utility (3). In the earlier example, it would also lead me to buy used, as that has the highest possible utility (6). Thus, the earlier example actually gets the same results from either the maximin or the maximax strategy. In the later example, the maximax strategy leads to buying used, whereas the maximin does not. So, the principles can conflict with one another, and, ultimately, the decision of which principle to use will turn on broader factors, such as whether it is more important to take risks or to avoid them.

⑮

INFORMAL FALLACIES

A *fallacy* is a defective argument. A *formal fallacy* is an invalid deductive argument: It is an argument the form (structure) of which does *not* guarantee that if the premises are true, then the conclusion must be true as well. An *informal fallacy,* or material fallacy, is an argument that fails to support its conclusion because of a defect in its content. This defect can have to do with problems of linguistic structure (fallacies of ambiguity), or relevance of the evidence for the conclusion (fallacies of relevance), or when more is assumed by the premises than is warranted (fallacies of presumption), or they may be weak inductive arguments (fallacies of weak induction). As we shall see, in many cases the difference between an acceptable argument and an informal fallacy is that, in the latter case, one of its premises is false.

15.1 FALLACIES OF AMBIGUITY

Fallacies of ambiguity are defective arguments based on multiple meanings of words or poor sentence construction. While these ambiguities might arise in many sentences, there must be an argument for there to be fallacy.

An *equivocation* is a fallacious argument in which the meaning of a word shifts from one premise to the next or from one of the premises to the conclusion such that each statement is true given one meaning of the word and false given the other.[1] For example:

All cats are small domestic animals.
All lions are cats.
Therefore, all lions are small domestic animals.

The first premise is true with respect to house cats (*Felis cattus*). It is false if *cat* is used in a more general sense for any members of the family *Felidae*. The second premise is true with respect to the more general notion of *cat*. It is false if *cat* is taken to mean a domestic animal of the genus and species *Felis cattus*. The argument uses the word *cat* in two senses; it *equivocates* on the word *cat*. If the conclusion were to follow from the premises, the term *cat* would have to remain constant. So, the argument commits the fallacy of equivocation.

Here's another equivocation:

If Dan is an author of this book, then he's a Flage. If Dan is a FLAGE, then he's a flexible lightweight agile guided experiment (an anti-missile missile). So, if Dan is an author of this book, then he's a flexible lightweight agile guided experiment (an anti-missile missile).

A fallacy of *amphiboly* is based on a loosely constructed sentence. Because of the loose sentence construction, it can be understood in more than one way, and there is a shift in meaning when going from the premises to the conclusion. Sometimes a poorly constructed sentence is the occasion on which a reader or hearer draws a false conclusion. For example:

In 2001, I received a memo reading, "We are going to commemorate the one-hundredth anniversary of Giuseppe Verdi's death at James Madison University." I was surprised, since I didn't know that Verdi had ever been at JMU, let alone died there. Then I remembered that JMU wasn't founded until 1908. In reaching the conclusion, my argument committed the fallacy of amphiboly. (What they had meant to say was, "We, at James Madison University, are going to commemorate the one-hundredth anniversary of Giuseppe Verdi's death.")

Here is another:

At 8:00 A.M. EST on November 17, 2003, a news report stated, "Today Arnold Schwarzenegger becomes California's thirty-sixth governor in six hours." Wow! They really go through governors in California!

The news report meant to say, "In six hours, Arnold Schwarzenegger will become California's thirty-sixth governor." As it is stated, one could take it to mean that California had gone through thirty-six governors in six hours, which is the meaning assumed by the conclusion.

The fallacy of *accent* can be committed in either of two ways. One way is to take a common statement and emphasize certain words in such a way as to change the meaning. For example:

> It's a general principle that you should get all the education you can. So, I don't have to go on to school.

A second way the fallacy can be committed is by shifting the meaning of a statement by quoting it only partly or out of context. For example:

> Assume Berndt argued that the sole justification for military action is self-defense, indicating that attack from a foreign power is a necessary condition for deeming an action self-defense. In the course of argument he remarked, "Some would claim that there are cases in which a preemptive attack is justified, but ..." Rolf responded, "National security requires that we be constantly vigilant. This might mean that in some cases we must attack before we are attacked. Even Berndt says, 'there are cases in which a preemptive attack is justified.'"

> By law, criminals in the United States must be treated very well. For the Eighth Amendment to the U.S. Constitution requires that "... bail shall not be required, nor ... fines imposed, nor ... punishments inflicted."

While Rolf quotes Berndt's words, Berndt used the words to introduce a position he was going to argue against. In the second example, the word "excessive" is deleted before "bail" and "fines," and the words "cruel and unusual" are deleted before "punishments."

Division is an argument from a property of a whole to a property of a part or from a property of a class of objects to a property of an object in that class. *Sometimes* such an argument is wholly justified: "My car weighs fewer than 3,000 pounds. So, the engine in my car weighs fewer than 3,000 pounds." In many cases it is not:

> According to the American Automobile Association, the cars on the road today are safer than they were ten years ago. So, my 1952 Ford is safer than it was ten years ago.

It might be true that, as a group, the cars on the road today are safer than the cars of a decade ago, but it *does not* follow from that that any individual car is safer than it was ten years ago. Again:

> $\Delta\Delta\Omega$ sorority is the richest sorority on campus. Donna is a member of $\Delta\Delta\Omega$. So, Donna is one of the richest women on campus.

The fact that the organization is wealthy does not entail that any given member of the organization is wealthy.

Composition is the mirror image of division. Composition argues from a property of a part to a property of a whole or from a property of a member of a class to a property of the class. In many cases it is fallacious:

> Mrs. Rich is one of the wealthiest people in town. So, the Southside Garden Club, of which Mrs. Rich is a member, is one of the wealthiest clubs in town.

There might be reasons to believe that the Southside Garden Club is wealthy or that it is composed primarily of wealthy members—perhaps wealthy people tend to congregate in the same social clubs—but the fact that Mrs. Rich is a member *by itself* does not show that the club is wealthy. Perhaps Mrs. Rich is a philanthropist who endowed a club for the less fortunate.

Of course, there are perfectly legitimate arguments from composition as well:

> The hard drive in my computer weighs more than twelve ounces. So my computer weighs more than twelve ounces.

And there are cases in which it might be hard to tell:

> I just replaced the hard drive in my five-year-old computer. The new hard drive cost $300. So my computer is worth at least $300.

15.2 FALLACIES OF RELEVANCE

An argument provides reasons to believe that its conclusion is true. If they are *good* reasons, they must be pertinent. The fallacies of relevance concern cases in which the reason given to accept a statement is not pertinent to the truth or falsehood of the statement it is alleged to support.

A fallacious *appeal to force* (*argumentum ad baculum*) contains an improper or inappropriate threat. Often, the argument is enthymematic:

Boss: You should contribute to the United Way. After all, you're currently employed.

Spelled out, the argument would look like this:

If you want to remain employed, you will give to the United Way.
You want to remain employed.
Therefore, you will give to the United Way.

The threat is inappropriate since *no one's* job description includes the requirement that one contribute to the United Way. Here is another example:

The boss said, "So you think you should inform the IRS that there are 'accounting irregularities' at our company. Go ahead. Do whatever you believe is necessary. Of course, if you talk to the IRS, I'll inform your husband of your 'matrimonial irregularities' with Mr. Drew."

Blackmail might convince one to act in a certain way, but it is never an acceptable basis for an argument.

There are occasions when apparently threatening discourse is not an inappropriate method of persuasion. Law enforcement is an example.

When one replies to an argument, one must show either that one or more of the premises is false or that the reasoning itself is faulty. The fallacy of *personal attack* (*argumentum ad hominem*) is committed when, in a reply to an argument, the arguer is attacked rather than the argument.[2] There are three types of personal attack:

Abusive: In the abusive form, the arguer's character is attacked:
Jessica has argued that capital punishment should be abolished. But Jessica is a known liar. So her argument should be rejected.

Even if Jessica has a reputation for "stretching the truth," this does not mean that she based her argument on false premises.

Circumstantial: In the circumstantial form, some aspect of the circumstances in which the arguer finds him- or herself is given as a reason to suggest that the argument is merely a rationalization:

Professor Jones has argued that the faculty deserve a pay raise. But Professor Jones would benefit from such a raise. So, you can't take his argument seriously.

Professor Jones might have a vested interest in pay raises for professors, but that fact does not show that the premises of his argument are false.

In her recent paper, Professor Smith argued that there are circumstances in which the death penalty is warranted. This view is inconsistent with her paper, "Death Penalty? Never!" published just ten years ago. Because her conclusions are inconsistent, we have no reason to take her arguments seriously.

Inconsistency is a serious charge. If a person reaches inconsistent conclusions *within a single work*, this is sufficient to show that there are serious problems with the work. On the other hand, if Professor Smith published two papers that reach inconsistent conclusions, this only shows that both arguments cannot be sound. In particular, it does not show that the arguments in the more recent paper are unsound.

Tu quoque (literally "you too"): The *tu quoque* form of the fallacy points to an inconsistency between the conclusion of a person's argument and that person's behavior:

You have argued that I should not drink beer. But you drink over a six-pack every day. So there's no reason to accept your argument.

Reverend, you tell us that we should be concerned with the welfare of the homeless. But you haven't turned the parsonage into a homeless shelter. So I see no reason to accept your arguments.

In both of these cases there is an apparent inconsistency between a person's arguments or claim and his or her actions. The fact that one does not follow one's own advice might show shortcomings of character, but it *does not* show either that the argument for a conclusion is weak or that a claim is false.

The general form of the fallacy of *mob appeal (argumentum ad populum)* is:

If believing that p is true makes one "feel good" (loved, accepted, important, special, virtuous, etc.), then p is true.
Believing that p is true makes one "feel good."
Therefore, p is true.

Such arguments are common in politics and advertising. Many activities at political conventions or rallies can have more of an emotional appeal than an appeal to reason. Insofar as they are arguments based on emotion, they are instances of mob appeal. Sometimes it takes the form of "snob appeal," suggesting that the reader or hearer is special and deserves some wonderful thing.

The movers and shakers of our town are all buried in Oak Ridge Cemetery. When it's your time, don't you want to be buried there too?

Being buried where a number of famous people are buried might make one feel important, but that's probably not a good basis for choosing a cemetery.

There is a general moral principle that maintains that one ought to help those who are less fortunate than oneself. The fallacy of *appeal to pity* (*argumentum ad misericordiam*) is an appeal to an *emotion*. Emotions are not propositions, and, therefore, cannot function in arguments. Further, it is an appeal to the emotion of pity in a situation when the above moral principle would not apply. For example:

Student: You have to let me take an incomplete in your class. If I don't get an incomplete, I'll fail your class and be expelled from school.

The fallacy of *accident* occurs when a general principle is applied in a situation in which the principle does not apply. Typically, there is a conflict between two principles and the arguer chooses the weaker principle. For example:

It's a general principle that one should tell the truth. So, if you're hiding Jews from the Nazis, a member of the Gestapo comes to your door and asks, "Are you hiding any Jews?" you should answer, "Yes" and tell him where they are.

One should always help people in distress. So, I should help my friend who finds answering the examination questions stressful.

We often argue from general principles. Who could doubt that Socrates is a mortal, given that all humans are mortals and Socrates is a human? Sometimes, however, such arguments are based on widely accepted but false beliefs about groups of individuals (stereotypes). *Stereotyping* is a fallacy in which such a stereotype is accepted as true and a conclusion is drawn from it. For example:

No redheads are even-tempered. Dan is a redhead. So Dan is not even-tempered.

All lawyers are greedy. So, Public Defender Smith is greedy.

In both cases, the general premise (the stereotype) is false.

The *genetic fallacy* is a variation on stereotyping based on a person's origins. For example:

No one from the rural South is intelligent. Joan is a person from the rural South. Therefore, Joan is not intelligent.[3]

Germans are warmongers. Albert Schweitzer was a German. So, Albert Schweitzer was a warmonger.

In both these cases, the general premise is false. In the second case, the conclusion is clearly false.

The *straw person* (*straw man*) fallacy occurs in the course of replying to an argument. Rather than attacking the premises or the reasoning itself, the object of attack is either an alleged, suppressed premise or a distortion of the conclusion. For example:

Assume Luigi argued that the government should take steps that would assure that persons between jobs could retain health insurance through their previous employer until such a time as they obtain another job. Solvig replies, "Luigi has argued that the government should take over the health insurance business. This is socialized medicine! Socialized medicine has been tried in Canada and Western Europe, and the result has been medical care is available only for the most serious cases. Those wanting elective or non-life-threatening surgery are put on a long waiting list or must travel outside the country to obtain treatment. We don't want that here. So, we must reject Luigi's argument."

Maggie proposed the following argument: "Terrorist threats have changed the way we need to look at civil liberties. Rights of speech and privacy will do us little good if we're all dead. Our most basic rights, the rights on which this great country was founded, are the rights to life and property. If retaining those rights means we need to allow more government surveillance of our lives, then reduced civil liberties are warranted. This is a reality we need to recognize, a reality that is already recognized in such democracies as Great Britain and Israel." Millie replied, "If we are to accept Maggie's conclusion, we must assume that a desirable end justifies any means to that end. By such a principle, preservation of life would allow that anyone at any time can be locked in a solitary prison cell to protect his or her life. But that's absurd! So, we must reject Maggie's argument."

In the first argument, Solvig distorts Luigi's conclusion. Luigi had made the modest claim that the government should pass legislation that would allow people to retain health insurance between jobs, which is far short of the socialized medicine Solvig suggested. In the second argument, Maggie suggested that certain civil liberties might need to be limited to protect life and property. Millie suggests that Maggie's argument rests on a far broader principle than Maggie employs.

A *red herring* is like a straw person insofar as it is a fallacious reply to an argument. It differs from a straw person, however, insofar as it attempts to distract the reader or hearer from the original argument: It "replies" by shifting the issue. For example:

> Assume Dr. Mendez argued that the local factory is unsafe and should be closed temporarily for repairs. Homer replies, "That factory is the largest employer in town. If it is closed, the entire town will be thrown into economic depression. We can't afford that! So we must reject Dr. Mendez's argument."

> Reverend Schmidt has argued that Christian doctrine requires that we aid the poor. But our building is in desperate need of repair. We need an education director to assure that our children receive proper religious training. And we, as a church, really should provide funds to support the Retired Is Not Dead group's mission trip to Hawaii. (Ten nights at the Marriott Ko'Olina Beach Club does not come cheap!) So we must reject Rev. Schmidt's argument.

Notice that in the first argument, the issue had been safety, but the "reply" focused on economics. In the second, the issue is giving to the poor, and the "reply" concerns other ways to spend money at the church.

If one follows an argument closely—regardless of whether it is an inductive or a deductive argument—one can usually anticipate the conclusion that is supported by the premise. An argument commits the fallacy of *irrelevant conclusion* (*ignoratio elenchi*; *non sequitur*) if a conclusion is reached that bears little resemblance to the conclusion that is supported by the premises. For example:

> All humans are mortals.
> All Greeks are humans.
> So, all Greeks are philosophers.

> A lot of people have put in a lot of work on this project.
> Therefore, the conclusions they have reached are correct.

15.3 FALLACIES OF PRESUMPTION

Fallacies of presumption occur when arguments make assumptions that are not warranted by the context in which they are found. In some cases, the premises assume the conclusion of the argument. In other cases, they assume that all the relevant information has been presented.

An argument *begs the question* if it assumes the conclusion of an argument as a premise. Sometimes the wording of the premise and conclusion differ, but the meaning of the two propositions is the same. Here are a couple examples:

Marie Antoinette was a queen, for she was a female monarch.

How can one teach without knowing something beforehand and without having been taught? A teacher must know and first be taught in what he teaches others.[4]

Notice that in the first example, "female monarch" and "queen" are synonymous. In the second, Luther's rhetorical question says the same as the premise that supposedly provides evidence for its truth.

Often it is in the course of a chain of arguments that the question is begged. This is called *arguing in a circle*: The premise of an earlier argument is the conclusion of a later argument. Here are a couple examples:

We know that everything the Bible says is true, since it is the inspired word of God. And we know that the Bible is the inspired word of God, since everything the Bible says is true.

College-age student to parent: "You should support my lifestyle at college because we all know that not all learning occurs in the classroom. And how do we know that not all learning occurs in the classroom? You wouldn't support my lifestyle at college if it did.

Notice that the first argument both assumes and concludes that the Bible is the inspired word of God. The second argument assumes and concludes that the parents should support the student's lifestyle at college.

There are also *question-begging epithets*. If Smith is charged with armed robbery and the prosecutor refers to her as "that crook Smith," the word "crook" begs the question of Smith's guilt.

Many of the questions we ask are complex; that is, they assume that another question has already been answered. "Where were you on Saturday night?" assumes that the person questioned was *somewhere* on Saturday night, and that is a reasonable assumption. The fallacy of *complex question* occurs when the question is loaded—the answerer is placed in a bad light however she answers—or the answer to the presumed question is false. A complex question *as such* is not a fallacy, since it's not an argument. But insofar as it provides the basis for an argument, it is included in the list of informal fallacies. For example:

> Boss: Where did you come up with this harebrained scheme?
> Employee: The idea came to me while I was reading Popular Mechanics.
> Boss: Ah ha! So you admit it's a harebrained scheme. We're going to have to make some changes around here!

> "When did you stop cheating on your income taxes?"

The first complex question assumes it was a harebrained scheme. The second complex question assumes there was a time when the person asked cheated on her income taxes. Neither assumption was warranted.

One does not typically develop all the arguments on each side of an issue, but, if a decision is to be made regarding an issue, the supporter of one side should not knowingly withhold evidence that does not support her case. If an arguer knowingly withholds relevant evidence, her argument commits the fallacy of *suppressed evidence*. For example:

> For the relief of headache pain, take potassium cyanide: You'll never have a headache again.

The relevant bit of evidence that is suppressed is that anyone who takes potassium cyanide dies.

A *false dichotomy* is a disjunctive syllogism with a false disjunctive premise. For example:

> Either you'll vote for the Republicans or for the Democrats. You've told me you won't vote for the Democrats. So, you'll be supporting the Republican Party.

At best, there is no guarantee that the disjunctive premise is true. Even if one vowed not to support the Democrats, one might support an independent candidate or not vote at all.

15.4 FALLACIES OF WEAK INDUCTION

Inductive arguments provide limited evidence for the truth of their conclusions. Some inductive arguments are stronger than others. The fallacies of weak induction are common ways in which inductive arguments fail.

The fallacy of *appeal to authority* or *appeal to illegitimate authority* is an appeal to an alleged authority that lacks credentials. We all make appeals to authority all the time, and many of them are legitimate. Students have good reason to believe (most) of what their teachers claim within their areas of expertise since they are trained in the area. When someone makes a claim outside his or her area of expertise, the reliability of his or her claim is far less certain. For example, if an actor or sports personality appears in a commercial, one has little reason to believe that he or she has expertise regarding the product endorsed.

What alleged authorities are illegitimate? Here is a partial list:

- Persons speaking outside their areas of expertise. Examples: Famous people in commercials; actors speaking on political issues; religious leaders talking about scientific issues.
- Tradition. Example: Supporting a certain political party because it is traditional in one's family, that is, taking tradition as such as a reason to believe that the views of the political party are worthy of support.
- Rumor. Examples: Rumors or gossip that spread from mouth to mouth; appeals to unnamed studies: If someone claims that "numerous studies show . . ." one needs to investigate the studies to determine *whether* they are to be trusted.

An *appeal to ignorance* is an argument of one of the two following forms:

We do not know that some proposition p is true.
Therefore, p is false.

We do not know that p is false.
Therefore, p is true.

If one does not know whether a proposition is true or false, it is wise to suspend judgment regarding the proposition's truth value. But from the fact that p is not known to be true (false), it does not follow that p is false (true). If you have any question, consider the following argument made in 1850:

We do not know that human beings can fly to the moon.
Therefore, human beings cannot fly to the moon.

It might have been over a century later before the lunar landing, but it was no less *possible* in 1850 than in 1969.

There are cases, however, when it is reasonable to accept what appeals to be an appeal to ignorance. If an expert in a field claims that there is no evidence that some phenomenon *in her field of expertise* occurred or could occur, one has some reason to believe that her negative claim is true.

A *hasty generalization* (converse accident) is an inductive generalization based on a very limited number of instances, particularly instances that are atypical. If I claimed that Chrysler does not make reliable cars because my 1981 Dodge Omni was not reliable, I would be guilty of a hasty generalization. My car was only one car made by Chrysler Corporation, and it was probably atypical.

The fallacy of *false cause* is a causal argument based on a false causal claim. Superstitions are common instances of the fallacy of false cause. If I claimed that a black cat crossed in front of my car this morning and that caused the entire day to be unlucky, I probably would be guilty of the fallacy of false cause. Even in the following case, the black cat would not be the whole cause:

I was driving to work. This black cat ran in front of my car. I swerved to miss it, lost control of my car, and slammed into a tree. I spent three weeks in the intensive care unit of the hospital, and even now, three years later, I still don't have full use of my left arm.

The cause of the person's bad luck was not the cat; it was his reaction to the cat running in front of his car. Or:

Gene Siskel was a movie critic, and he died of cancer. Joel Siegel was a movie critic, and he died of cancer. Roger Ebert is a movie critic, and he's been battling cancer for the past several years. So, if you don't want to get cancer, don't be a movie critic.

It is highly unlikely that being a movie critic causes cancer.

A *slippery slope* argument is a series of causal arguments. Typically, things start rather innocently and become progressively worse as one proceeds down the slope. The following is a common fallacious slippery slope argument:

> You should not drink beer because if you drink beer, you'll try wine. If you try wine, you'll try various liqueurs. If you try liqueurs, you'll try hard liquor, like whiskey and brandy, and you'll end up as a hopeless alcoholic. It will all be from a little glass of beer.

There might be good reasons not drink, but none is supported by this argument: Drinking one kind of alcoholic beverage does not cause one to drink another. If each of the causes obtains, however, a slippery slope argument is *not* fallacious. The following argument is a slippery slope argument, but there is reason to believe that each of the causal claims is true, so there is reason to believe that it is *not* a fallacious slippery slope:

> You shouldn't drive slower than the posted minimum speed limit on the interstates. If you drive slower than the posted minimum speed, sooner or later someone will rear-end you. If someone rear-ends you while driving slower than the posted minimum speed, you will be found at fault for the accident. If you're found at fault, your insurance rates will rise. If your insurance rates rise, you will have less disposable income for enjoyable activities. So, you shouldn't drive slower than the posted minimum speed limits on the interstates.

A slippery slope is *fallacious* only if at least one of the causal claims is false.

Notice that a slippery slope argument is fundamentally a hypothetical syllogism in which the conditional statements make causal claims. In the case of a fallacious slippery slope, at least one of the causal claims is false. Since one is encouraged *not* to start down the slope, it also involves a case of denying the antecedent. While denying the antecedent is formally fallacious, in a causal situation, it is a reasonable assumption that if the cause is absent, the effect will be as well—although a given effect often can arise from a different cause. So, in the case of a slippery slope argument in which each of the premises is true, avoiding the initial cause provides some—but not conclusive—evidence that the effect will not occur. If all the causal claims are true, avoiding the initial cause gives good inductive reasons to believe that one will also avoid the effect. For example, the following is a nonfallacious slippery slope argument:

> *You don't want to tailgate on the highway. If you tailgate, the chances are good that you will eventually run into a car that is ahead of you. If you run into a car ahead of you, there is a good chance that you'll be injured, and your auto insurance rates are almost certain to rise. If your auto insurances rates rise, you'll have less money for more enjoyable purposes. So, you shouldn't tailgate.*

There are any number of reasons why your insurance rates might rise even if you do not tailgate, but this slippery slope gives you good reasons to avoid tailgating.

A *weak analogy* is an analogical argument in which the objects compared are different in a significant way (are disanalogous) such that the conclusion of the argument is poorly supported. For example:

> *A compact Chevy is like a Cadillac insofar as both are made by General Motors. A Cadillac is a luxurious car. So, a compact Chevy is also a luxurious car.*

A compact Chevy is a relatively inexpensive car. A Cadillac is a relatively expensive car. Luxury is expensive. Here is another:

> *Blue Ridge Community College is like Harvard insofar as it provides a strong core curriculum. Harvard graduates have little trouble finding jobs in their chosen fields. So Blue Ridge Community College graduates have little trouble finding jobs in their chosen fields.*

While Blue Ridge Community College is said to be a very good *community college*, it differs from Harvard in more ways than it is similar.

NOTES

1. When discussing categorical syllogisms, this is known as the fallacy of four terms. It violates the first rule in section 5.2 in chapter 5.

2. If one looks back at the criteria for evaluating testimony in chapter 4, one will notice some correlation between the occasions the criteria suggest skepticism in terms of a person offering testimony and personal attack. For example, if a person is of less-than-sterling character, one might be skeptical of that person's testimony. If a person is biased, one might be skeptical of the person's testimony. These are issues that should be taken into account in evaluating the probable reliability of a person's testimony. In the case of a personal attack, either of these is given as a reason

to reject the person's *argument* without any examination of the argument's strength.

3. Sometimes the genetic fallacy is coupled with personal attack: "Ivan argued that . . . But Ivan is from the Deep South (where no one is very bright). So, we must reject Ivan's argument."

4. Martin Luther, *Luther: Lectures on Romans*, trans. Wilhelm Pauck, The Library of Christian Classics, Volume 15 (Philadelphia: Westminster Press, 1966), 54.

⓰

CRITICAL WRITING: AN AUDIENCE-CENTERED APPROACH TO CRITICAL THINKING

Critical thinking is a process of reasoning by which one can decide what to believe and do. Through such processes, individuals develop their own perspectives of the world around them. In many cases, individuals also wish to share the opinions and ideas resulting from their critical thinking with others. Such sharing, in turn, is often done through writing. This writing could take the form of everything from a blog posting to a newspaper article to a formal research paper. In all cases, the effective use of writing to transfer ideas requires authors to think critically about communication situations. If, for example, Author A wishes to discuss the topic of Senator Smith's approval ratings (see section 8.1 in chapter 8) with other individuals, that writer must think critically about how much a particular audience of readers already knows about that topic. Only through such reflection can a writer determine what ideas will require an in-depth explanation of all premises and what ideas an audience probably knows and accepts. Such an understanding of audience is crucial to providing the context readers need to understand the meaning the writer wishes to convey. And, as noted in chapter 1, providing this context is essential to determining the correct meaning of an individual statement or an overall argument.

As a result of this relationship between context and meaning, the sharing of ideas via writing often shifts the thought process from the realm of ideas to that of audience. This shift means that individuals must now think critically about how to present written ideas in a way that a reader—or an *audience*—will understand. Such audience assessment is often a matter of formulating effective critical questions that help prospective authors better understand audience expectations related to a particular written document. In the previously mentioned case of Author A, such a critical question might be "How much does my intended audience already know about Senator Smith's situation?" This process of using critical thinking to guide writing practices is known as *critical writing*, and it is essential to sharing ideas effectively through written texts. As a result, critical writing places a special focus on two of the four major critical thinking questions presented in the introduction of this book:

- What reasons are there to believe that a statement/premise/claim is true?
- How good are the reasons to believe the statement/premise/claim is true?

This chapter uses the Aristotelian concept of rhetoric to introduce readers to the critical writing process. In so doing, the chapter also provides an overview of how individuals can use critical writing concepts to convey information to different reading audiences.

16.1 EXAMINING CRITICAL WRITING: A RHETORICAL APPROACH

Critical writing, like critical thinking, is based on the notion of critique. In critical thinking, one engages in an internal/mental critique of the efficacy of arguments presented by others. In critical writing, this perspective shifts, and one must now think critically about how to present effective arguments to others. As a result, critical writing, like critical thinking, is often associated with the notion of *argument*—that is, one presents a structured argument as to why his or her particular opinion (i.e., a critique of an idea) is credible and worthy of the consideration of other individuals. The critical writing process thus involves stating a premise and then setting out to prove that premise in a way that will effectively win readers over to a writer's point of view. In this way, critical writing focuses on the idea of *soundness*—or providing solid evidence for supporting an idea or conclusion (see chapter 5). Creating critical written arguments requires writers to understand audience expectations related to what constitutes a legitimate premise, what constitutes legitimate evidence for supporting that premise, and how an overall argument should be structured to be considered persuasive. Critical writing thus requires authors to closely consider what chapter 4 notes as the relevant set of criteria an audience expects to encounter in order to accept a claim or an opinion as "true." For these reasons, critical writing requires individuals to think critically about the audience with which they will share information. Only through such reflection can a writer hope to understand the criteria an audience associates with creating believable arguments in relation to a particular topic.

As the objective of critical writing is to convince others of the believability of an author's opinions or ideas, the overall process is persuasive in nature. For this reason, approaches to critical writing often involve the use of *rhetoric*, which is commonly defined as the art of persuasion. First developed some 2,000 years ago by the Greek philosopher and teacher Aristotle, rhetoric provides a framework for understanding how to craft persuasive arguments by addressing audience expectations. Aristotle's ideas on rhetoric, moreover, are linked to his critical thinking notions of syllogistic or enthymematic arguments as presented in his treatise *On Rhetoric* and as summarized in chapter 5 of this text.

While Aristotle's original ideas focused on spoken presentations, these same ideas have also proven effective in the development of persuasive written texts. Terms such as "presentation" are therefore used to describe both oral and written displays of information, for both "present" ideas to a particular audience.

Today, Aristotle's ideas on rhetoric and presentations can serve as a framework for critical decision making related to written communication. By using Aristotle's concepts of the forum (presentation situation), ethos (credibility of information), and the special topics (kind of information presented), writers can begin to understand how audiences might perceive various written documents. Writers can then use these insights to ask focused questions and to develop effective written arguments for such audiences. Thus, Aristotle's rhetorical concepts can provide writers with a more effective means of sharing the results of their critical thinking with different audiences.

16.2 SELECTING THE APPROPRIATE FORUM

The first and perhaps the most important step to presenting an effective written argument is to determine the type of document (written text) the author will use to convey information. From a rhetorical perspective, this factor of type or kind is often referred to as the *forum* in which information is presented. From an oral presentation perspective, the forum is the setting or context in which one voices ideas. From a written communication perspective, the forum is the type of written document (print or electronic) an author uses to convey information. Thus, written forums are often parallel to the genres used to convey textual information. These forums/genres include things such as letters, e-mails, research reports, websites, newspaper articles, and blogs. Readers, in turn, use these forums to achieve different objectives. The readers of a newspaper article, for example, use that forum to remain updated on current events. The readers of an e-mail message rely on that forum to gain information from a specific person, and readers of instruction manuals expect those texts to provide information on how to perform a particular process.

According to this perspective, the most important factor is that readers associate each forum with a particular *purpose*. Those readers then expect authors to provide the specific information needed to achieve the purpose associated with that forum. Within this framework, authors who present ideas and information in a way that meets these audience expectations will tend to be viewed positively by readers. Authors who do not address the expected purpose of a forum, however, can incur the displeasure of readers. This displeased audience might not read an overall document or might disregard an author's opinion because of this failure to meet perceived forum expectations. Thus, from an overall critical thinking perspective, one could say that the forum brings with it the criteria that audiences use for assessing the effectiveness of a presentation. (See the introduction and chapter 4 for an overview of criteria and audience expectations related to the general critical thinking process.)

Consider the following situation: You discover that you cannot get your car to start and none of the electrical features on your car seem to work. To try to figure out the cause of the problem—and to try to determine a possible solution—you open the owner's manual for your car and turn to the section titled "Electrical Systems." Instead of finding a brief discussion of how such systems operate and instructions on how to troubleshoot related problems (what you expect in that forum), you encounter a scientific research report on how temperature variations over the course of time can affect the electromagnetic properties of different machines. While this discussion might be interesting and well written, it is not the particular kind of information you need at that time. Moreover, it does not address the purpose for which you decided to use the owner's manual in the first place. Rather, there is a stark disconnect in terms of the criteria the author and the audience are using to assess the effectiveness of the argument or presentation in the forum of this owner's manual.

As a result of this mismatch, your initial response to this written information might be confusion, frustration, or anger. It is also highly unlikely that you would be in the frame of mind needed to appreciate the qualities of the information presented on how temperature variations can affect electromagnetic properties. In this way, failing to meet the forum expectations of a reader can affect how that reader reacts to a written argument—no matter how well researched and well written that argument might be.

For this reason, the very first critical thinking step in the overall writing process is self-reflection. Specifically, one needs to think critically about the objective he or she wishes to accomplish through writing. All authors should therefore begin the critical writing process by asking the all-important question:

What purpose or objective do I wish to achieve through my writing?

The answer to this question is the initial step toward selecting the forum, or the genre, best suited to achieving the author's objective for sharing information. If, for example, the answer is "to provide a critique of a book I've read," then the forum best suited for achieving that purpose is a book review. If, however, the purpose is to comment critically on recent events in one's hometown, then the forum best suited for that objective might be an editorial in the local newspaper. Thus, forum selection is a matter of aligning the criteria that audiences associate with effective arguments with those the author intends to use in presenting an argument.

It should be noted that individuals within a population can vary in terms of the expectations they have for a particular forum. As noted in chapter 1, each individual brings his or her own context to the process of interpreting what words or phrases mean. Writers must therefore often think critically about who the average reader or audience member might be and what expectations that person might have in relation to a particular forum.

Perhaps the best way to understand such an audience is to review and analyze other written materials designed for that audience. (In fact, scholars of rhetoric have long noted that one of the best ways to devise a strategy for effective presentations is to review the successful presentations of others.) Writers might therefore wish to review examples of a particular forum or genre before deciding if that forum is best suited in terms of the purpose the writer wishes to achieve. So, before drafting a newspaper editorial to share one's opinions on local events, a writer should review previous editorials in local newspapers to confirm that readers associate this forum with that particular purpose.

16.3 ESTABLISHING PRESENTATION OBJECTIVES

As noted earlier, the objective of critical writing is to share the results of the author's critical thinking process with readers and to do so in a way that can persuade readers that such ideas have merit. Thus, critical writing—like critical thinking—begins with stating a premise (i.e., an idea or opinion) and then presenting evidence to support that premise and construct a sound argument. (See the discussion of "sound arguments" in chapter 2.) In many cases, however, authors become so wrapped up in presenting evidence that they forget to let readers know what the original premise, or objective, of their writing is. In this way, a written argument can take on the problematic form of the enthymematic arguments described in chapter 5. Yet without a clearly stated objective or purpose for why an author is presenting information, readers are left to guess at how to interpret the evidence contained in a document. Thus, the written argument falls victim to the problems of ambiguity discussed in chapter 1.

In some cases, the author makes the mistake of assuming the forum alone is enough to provide readers with the context needed to intuit the author's reason for presenting written information. While the forum is an effective tool for gauging what readers expect to take from a given document, it does not provide information on the specific objectives for which the author uses that forum. The forum of a book review, for example, brings with it the implicit notion that readers will use that forum to learn more about a particular book. Whether an author/reviewer liked a book, however, cannot be determined from that forum. Rather, this claim of like or dislike (the objective the author will try to prove through the genre of the book review) must be directly stated by the author who is using that genre.

Moreover, should an author fail to state such an objective explicitly and at the start of an overall presentation, readers might be unsure of how to interpret the evidence that the author presents at later points within the same document. (The problem again becomes one of ambiguity as noted in chapter 1.) If, for example, an author notes that "30% of all left-handed individuals score 90% or better on standardized tests," what exactly does that data mean? Without some overarching objective statement that lets the reader know what point the author is trying to prove in this paper, the statement of "30%" could be a positive or a negative factor. An overarching statement that lets the reader know that the objective of the paper is "to reveal that left-handed persons perform better on tests than right-handed persons" provides the reader with some context for how to interpret such evidence.

Sentences that sum up an author's purpose or objective for presenting information in a particular forum/document are known as *thesis statements*, and they provide readers with a context for interpreting information. The thesis is thus the initial premise that provides the context that audiences use to determine how well evidence supports a particular conclusion. (See the discussion of "arguments" in section 2.1 in chapter 2 for a more in-depth discussion of this process in critical thinking.) As the thesis statement establishes such context, it is important that these statements occur at an early point in an overall document and ideally in the first, or introductory, section of that document.

Additionally, the more direct the statement of purpose or objective, the lesser the likelihood that the author's purpose will be misinterpreted by readers. For example, the statement "This paper examines the writings of Jack London" is quite vague—or ambiguous—and does not let the reader know why the author thinks such an examination is important or what the objective of such an examination might be. However, the statement "This paper examines the writings of Jack London in order to reveal how his experiences in Alaska shaped the subject matter of his short stories" reduces ambiguity and provides the reader with a clear understanding of the nature of the examination the writer will undertake and why the writer will perform such an examination. Such a direct thesis statement also provides the reader with the context needed to understand how the author will use different pieces of information presented in the related paper. In the case of the Jack London example, should the reader later encounter a statement such as "This section examines London's short story 'To Build a Fire,'" that reader knows that this examination will focus on revealing how "To Build a Fire" relates to London's experiences in Alaska.

To provide readers with an effective thesis statement and thus an effective guide for how to read and interpret a particular presentation, an author next needs to ask the question:

What specific objective do I wish to accomplish by presenting information within this particular forum?

Once the author knows the answer to this question, he or she can draft a thesis statement that effectively and directly presents such an objective to readers. In so doing, the author provides the context for how readers should interpret the information presented in the rest of the overall document. A well-written thesis statement, moreover, can serve as a mechanism for determining what content should be included in a particular document. It can also contribute greatly to the initial sense of credibility authors generate for their arguments.

16.4 ESTABLISHING INITIAL CREDIBILITY

The notion of "credibility" often blends the idea of acceptance with truth. That is, when we say something is "credible," we accept that the item in question is true (see chapter 2). From a critical writing perspective, credibility is essential, for individuals will read, consider, and even agree with written arguments they consider credible. However, the moment an author fails to meet such credibility expectations, readers will begin to discount certain points or even stop reading. Thus, from a critical writing perspective, convincing others to follow and accept a written argument becomes a matter of creating and maintaining a sense of credibility throughout an overall presentation. Authors also need to maintain this perception of credibility if they wish readers to accept the ideas and the arguments presented in that document. From a rhetorical perspective, this notion of credibility is often referred to as *ethos*, and meeting and maintaining an audience's expectations of ethos is central to sharing information effectively with others.

In all arguments, the author begins with a premise—a claim, an opinion, or an idea—that serves as the focus or objective for an overall argument. The author next presents evidence that supports that initial premise. From the perspective of a written argument, this premise is generally the thesis statement the author uses to introduce the overall idea or opinion he or she is trying to prove in a given document. After this thesis is stated, the author similarly needs to present information that will support that thesis. If, for example, one's premise/thesis is that left-handed persons do better on standardized tests than right-handed persons, the author might follow that thesis with a discussion of how testing results reveal that left-handed individuals, on average, seem to score better on the SAT and the ACT tests than do right-handed individuals. In essence, the author uses this presentation of evidence to support the idea that his or her thesis is sound (see chapter 2).

According to this model, the thesis statement can generate both initial interest and an initial sensation of credibility. If a reader finds an author's initial thesis plausible—or what is called *modest* in chapters 8 and 10—(e.g.,

"Left-handed persons do better than right-handed persons on standardized tests" vs. "Left-handed persons are better than right-handed persons in every way"), then that reader is more likely to continue reading the overall paper and more likely to consider versus dismiss the arguments the author presents to support that thesis. Aristotle would say that the audience would be initially *predisposed* to view the related presentation as credible.

At this level, how a writer words a thesis statement can affect the degree of credibility with which one views the argument presented in the related document. As a general rule, the more specific the wording—or the more modest the claim—of the thesis, the more open an audience would be to considering that premise or thesis as credible (see chapters 8 and 10). For example, the thesis statement "Left-handed persons do better than right-handed persons on standardized tests" is rather specific, and this specificity provides individuals with a relatively manageable way to test this claim to see if it is true (e.g., compare the scores of equal numbers of left- and right-handed persons who took the same standardized test under the same conditions). The thesis "Left-handed persons are better than right-handed persons in every way," however, is so broad and so general—or so lacking in modesty—that it is almost impossible to prove as true. Can, for example, an individual account for every possible situation in which left-handed persons could display such superiority? This statement is also so broad that it could actually be contradictory (e.g., implied in this claim is the notion that left-handed persons should be better at using their right hands than all right-handed persons are).

Thus, using a thesis statement to create an initial sense of credibility requires the writer to ask two critical questions:

What exact or specific idea do I wish to prove in this written argument?

and

How should I word my thesis statement in order to present an initial premise my audience will consider credible?

At this point, an author should review his or her original thesis to determine how modest that statement is (e.g., is it too broad to believe?) or if that thesis contains any claims that could jeopardize the initial credibility of the overall argument. (See, for example, the discussion of emotionally charged terms in chapter 1.) The author might even wish to do a test of the thesis by having others read it and comment on the believability and acceptability of that statement. Once the author has reviewed and revised the thesis, that author is ready to begin selecting content—information, ideas, and opinions—to include in the overall presentation.

16.5 SCREENING CONTENT FOR INCLUSION

Many writers experience problems when determining how much and what kinds of information to use in a written argument. In many cases, the writer has done a considerable amount of research on an overall topic area and suddenly finds him- or herself with a mountain of data, opinions, or ideas related to that topic. The question becomes what content the author should include in the written argument and what should be excluded. This question is an important one, for as noted in chapter 3, "one of the nasty things about ordinary prose is it often contains extraneous information." The related answer is key, for presentations that contain nonessential or unrelated information can distract or confuse readers to the point that they stop reading. Yet presentations that do not present all the essential information expected by readers could fail to provide a strong enough case for an audience to accept an author's ideas or opinions. (As noted in chapter 2, this shortcoming is a problem inherent to many inductive arguments.)

By crafting a very specific and direct thesis statement, authors provide themselves with a mechanism for determining what content to include in a particular document. If a certain bit of information does not seem related to the specifics of the thesis statement, then that information should not be included in the related paper, for it doesn't contribute to proving the author's overall claim. Say, for example, the author's thesis is "This paper examines the writings of Jack London in order to reveal how his experiences in Alaska shaped the subject matter of his stories." In this context, a discussion of London's novella *The Scarlet Plague* would have little to contribute to the related paper, for the novella has nothing to do with Alaska (it focuses on a pandemic disease outbreak in the San Francisco Bay Area). Rather, such an extraneous discussion would likely distract readers from the central objective of the paper. For this reason, the topic of *The Scarlet Plague* should be excluded from this particular document.

In using the thesis statement to select content for an overall document, an author must repeatedly ask these questions:

Does this information contribute to my objective for writing this paper? If so, how does it contribute?

If the answer to the first question is yes and the answer to the second question is relatively easy and obvious, then chances are that the related information should be included in the overall paper. After content has been screened via the thesis statement, the author needs to engage in a new round of critical reflection—one that focuses on the sources of information used to support an argument.

16.6 CONSIDERING SOURCES OF INFORMATION

In many cases, writers rely on sources (e.g., newspaper or magazine articles, books, and websites) to provide statistics, values, or other kinds of information they use to support their opinions in a particular forum. Such sources, however, are not neutral. Rather, the individuals presenting information through such media are doing so for a specific purpose. As noted in chapter 8, different groups (e.g., political pollsters vs. clothing store pollsters) might treat the same information (e.g., the average height of a sample population in a survey) differently because of the varying presentation objectives of those groups. Audiences, moreover, tend to be aware of this factor and tend to view certain kinds of sources with a degree of skepticism depending on the audience and the source. This factor of perception is important, for it can influence how audiences react to supporting evidence drawn from certain sources.

In his discussion of ethos, Aristotle explains that an audience's perception of credibility is often linked to that audience's perception of the speaker presenting information. (From a broader critical thinking perspective, one might call this the degree of confidence an audience has in a particular speaker.) As a result, if an audience considers a particular source to be "noncredible" (i.e., low degree of confidence), that audience will often assume that all ideas presented by that source are also lacking in credibility, even when the information being presented is true. It is much like the famous story of the boy who cried wolf: The title character had developed such a reputation for lying about impending wolf attacks that when a real wolf did appear, no one believed him. (In this case, a low degree of audience confidence trumped the truth of the boy's final argument.) For this reason, critical writing requires authors to think critically about both how audiences might respond to certain information and how they might respond to sources of that information.

To understand how this association works, consider the following example: I believe that automobiles are inherently unsafe because I don't trust automotive manufacturers to consider a consumer's best interests when making cars. As a result of this belief, I am likely to view any research reported by the automotive manufacturing association with great skepticism. You then produce a written argument in which you advocate certain safety practices and in so doing cite the automotive manufacturing association as the primary source of the data you use to support your points and ideas. Because I do not trust the automotive manufacturing association, I believe the information you use to support your points is not credible, and thus your points are not worthy of my consideration, for they lack what I would consider to be legitimate support. As a result, I will likely view your overall thesis as noncredible, for you have failed to provide what I consider legitimate evidence to support that thesis. In such a situation, my preoccupation with the sources of your data distracts me from the logic of your argument and thus affects your ability to achieve the purpose of presenting that argument in writing. (In this case, my emotional response to the source of the information is strong enough to prompt me to disregard the logic of your presentation.)

For this reason, a crucial step in selecting information to support a written argument involves the sources of information one uses. As a writer conducts research and collects information for writing projects, that person therefore needs to ask the question:

How will my intended audience respond to information from this particular source?

The answer to this question should not be the automatic rejection of certain information—or even the rejection of the related source. (In fact, presenting an argument that appears to be too one-sided can also jeopardize an individual's credibility.) Rather, the author should look for other sources—ones the intended audience considers credible—that support the same ideas or confirm information found in the "questionable" source. The author should then mention both sources when presenting that information. By providing such confirmation, the author not only can use ideas and opinions from a wider range of sources but can also provide a more balanced presentation of information—one that further contributes to the author's credibility by helping that author appear objective in relation to a topic.

16.7 IDENTIFYING CONTENT AREAS

Once a writer has determined the forum best suited for sharing ideas, that person must next determine how to organize information within an overall document. Such organization is critical to the development of an argument that is both logical and easy to follow. (An author, for example, can draft very logical arguments that are written in such a complex fashion that it is virtually impossible for readers to follow the logic of the argument.) One way to achieve this goal is by organizing information into sections or chunks and then using a section heading to identify the contents of a particular section.

The question then becomes how to chunk information effectively within a forum. Ideally, the method should be one that complements an audience's purpose for reading or using a document. By organizing or chunking ideas according to the reader's expectations of the forum, the writer presents content in a manner that makes it easier for readers to locate and use desired (forum-specific) information. (To understand how these ideas relate to general critical thinking practices, see the discussion of indicator words in chapter 3.) This strategy also increases the chances that a reader will use a given document, for it has been tailored to that person's particular reading expectations.

Fortunately, Aristotle's ideas on rhetoric provide a mechanism for identifying topic areas related to a specific forum. The idea is that when an audience comes to a particular forum, that audience looks for certain, forum-specific topics—or kinds of information—essential to addressing the purpose of the forum (i.e., certain, forum-specific indicator words). So, for example, if students (audience) associate the forum/genre of a class syllabus with the purpose of providing information on how to behave and to succeed in a given class, they will automatically look for any information (i.e., indicator words) related to such behaviors. Such information could include topic areas like "attendance," "grading," and "assignments." Each of these areas is central to the purpose of the related forum (the syllabus). At the same time, the importance of each topic area is linked directly to that one particular kind of forum. That is, while students look for and recognize the importance of topics like "attendance," "grading," and "assignments" within the forum of a class syllabus, they would likely not recognize or necessarily care about the importance of these same topics within the context of a different forum—such as instructions on how to operate a cell phone. (In the case of cell phone instructions, such topics would be seen as nonessential, or extraneous, information that distracts readers from the purpose of making use of that forum.) Aristotle refers to these forum-specific topics (indicator words) as *special topics*, for their importance is unique, or special, to a particular genre of communication.

According to this approach, authors should not spread their discussion of a particular topic across various parts or passages of a document. In fact, doing so could create confusion as readers might need to flip back and forth in order to find all of the ideas related to a particular special topic. Instead, content should be organized into blocks of topic-specific information within a paper. Such an organizational system helps readers better understand the links between different ideas associated with a special topic area. (What in section 6.1 in chapter 6 is referred to as "relations among propositions.") It also helps readers locate information quickly should they wish to find a special kind of information within a particular document. Thus, organizing information into special topic categories helps readers find the context they need to achieve their purpose for using a particular document or forum. As a result, authors can use the special topics to identify and organize content in a way that meets audience expectations, encourages use/reading of that document, and contributes to the writer's credibility.

This particular approach means authors need to think critically about what kinds of specific information—special topics—readers expect to find in a particular kind of document. Thus, the next critical question to ask in the writing process is:

What kinds of specific information will my audience look for in this forum?

This question will help authors identify important themes or topics to address in their presentation; it also provides writers with a mechanism for organizing information into special topic categories. To confirm the special topics associated with a particular forum, authors can review examples of similar genres designed for the same reading audience. As special topics are linked to a particular forum (e.g., user instructions), writers should review several examples of the same forum/genre to determine what topics are repeated throughout that genre. Such repeated topics would be what readers expect to encounter when using that particular sort of document. In the case of instructions sets, for example, topics such as "needed materials" and "caution" would likely appear in all instructions sets as they relate to that forum's purpose—to provide information on how to perform a particular process. Such items would thus be special topics within that forum.

16.8 GROUPING INFORMATION FOR READERS

Once content has been selected, it must be organized into categories, or major topic areas, that will make it manageable for authors to raise and discuss particular points related to presenting a critical argument or assessment. To help readers locate such points within a forum, authors should use headings that identify the specific themes covered within a document. Such headings can help readers find information quickly, and they can provide readers with a context for understanding the information contained within a section that has a particular heading. (In essence, the author uses headings to create indicator words for that forum.)

Creating such a context through headings can further help readers understand how different bits of information contained within a section are related (i.e., they all relate back to the central theme or topic noted in the section's heading). For these reasons, the wording of a particular heading is of great importance and should not be chosen at random. Rather, such wording needs to both reflect the kind of information found in a particular section and suggest how that information relates to the central forum purpose for which readers are using a document.

In such cases, the special topics can serve as a guide, for the more closely headings reflect the special topics associated with a given forum, the more likely readers are to review passages of text associated with such headings. To return to the example of the syllabus, once the author has organized information into special topic areas—those of attendance, grades, and assignments—he or she should use headings that clearly and explicitly note that such information is contained in these areas. Such headings could read as "Attendance Policies," "Grading Criteria," and "Assignment Requirements." Each of these headings is unambiguous, and each heading lets readers find essential, forum-specific information quickly and easily. Moreover, by contributing to such use on a relatively surface level (i.e., headings are something one can read while skimming a document), the author establishes a sense of credibility with the reader by revealing an understanding of that reader's expectations of that forum.

For these reasons, prospective authors need to think critically about how they word the headings used to organize documents. In this case, the critical question the author needs to ask is:

What specific words or terms does my audience associate with this particular forum?

Those words or terms, in turn, should appear in the headings related to a particular topic area. By including such words in headings, authors increase the chances that materials will be read and that the overall document will prompt readers to view the document with an initial perception of credibility as it meets the reading expectations/forum expectations of that audience.

16.9 ORGANIZING INFORMATION WITHIN THE FORUM

Once content has been categorized into major topic areas and headings have been identified, writers next need to determine how such topic areas should be organized within the context of an overall document. Such organization, in turn, needs to be based on the audience's expectations related to credibility within a given forum. Addressing this factor requires the author to engage in critical thinking related to two different situations.

As noted in chapter 4, virtually every field has criteria that are used as guidelines for reaching decisions. Similarly, many field-specific forums bring with them very strict expectations of how information must be organized to help readers achieve the evaluative/decision-making purpose of that forum. Academic research articles, for example, often follow the format shown here:

Introduction	Provides an overview of the main ideas presented in the article
Review of the literature / past research on the topic	Presents information needed to understand the importance of the research
Methods used for conducting research	Describes how the author researched a particular topic and provides information needed to replicate and test the results
Results / findings	Displays data resulting from the research approach described in the previous section
Discussions	Presents the author's opinion of how to interpret and apply the results
Conclusion	Summarizes the main ideas covered in the article

All of these component parts are essential to achieving the objective for which the intended audience uses this genre (to learn about new research findings). Additionally, this particular order of topics is essential for helping readers accomplish the purpose for reading such an article. That is, earlier sections of the article provide information essential to understanding the ideas presented in later sections of that article. To understand the "Results/Findings," for example, one first needs to know what "Methods" were used to generate those results. Thus, the logic used to organize information in this forum is based not on what the writer wishes to prove but on what the reader wishes to accomplish in this forum. By rearranging the order of these parts, then, one would prevent readers from achieving this purpose and would thus dissuade them from considering information presented in such a nonconventional format.

For this reason, before individuals begin writing, they need to ask the question:

Does my audience expect information to be organized in a particular way within this genre?

The only way to answer this question is to review examples of a forum and look for patterns in how information is organized within that forum. In many cases, these standard forum expectations coincide with particular headings (i.e., special topic areas) found within a given genre of document. In doing a review of a forum, writers should review several examples of a particular genre to answer two important questions:

Is there a pattern in terms of the kinds of headings used in that forum?

and

Do those headings (major information areas) always appear in a particular order within that forum?

Authors can then use patterns they find as a guide for both how to organize their own presentation and how to word the headings used in that presentation.

In some instances, audiences might have a very open set of expectations related to how content is organized within a specific forum. While it is important for authors to address the expected special topics in these forums, the order in which those topics appear is completely up to the author. This lack of organizational expectation, however, does not mean that authors are free to present information in whatever order they wish. (Consider, for example, the comprehension problems that could occur if an author presented the parts of a syllogism in a random order.) Rather, a different rhetorical concept can serve as a guide for ordering such presentations.

Traditionally, the concept of *kairos* has been associated with timing. That is, the time at which a particular piece of information is presented within an argument plays a pivotal role in determining if that information and if the overall argument are accepted by a given audience. In some cases, kairos is determined by requirements of logic. In such cases, if a reader needs to

understand topic A before he or she can understand topic B, then in the related written argument, the author must present A first and then B. (To explain the concept of divorce, for example, the author must first make sure
the reader understands the prerequisite condition of marriage.)

In other cases, however, all information can appear to have equal importance and not need to be presented in a particular logical order. For example, arguing why peanut butter is better than jelly can involve the presentation of different facts that do not necessarily need to be presented in a
particular logical order to advocate a point. It is in these cases of equally important information that kairos becomes truly important.

In his discussions of rhetoric, Aristotle notes that persuasion (getting
someone to accept a particular idea) is often linked to predisposition (how
someone feels about a particular topic). Thus, the more positively predisposed someone is to an idea, the more likely that person is to accept that
idea. Accordingly, if writers begin an argument with a topic the audience is
negatively predisposed to (likely to reject), then that author essentially
taints how that audience will view all other information that follows that initial topic. The objective then becomes to keep the audience positively predisposed to what the author presents throughout a document. Doing so will
increase the chances the audience will accept what the author presents as
credible and agree with the author's points and the author's overall thesis.

For this reason, writers should begin their writing by presenting evidence
they know their audience will accept without problem. The author must
then try to maintain such a predisposition throughout the overall presentation. When organizing a written presentation, the author must therefore ask
the questions:

To which topics will my audience react positively?

and, conversely,

To which topics will my audience react negatively?

Clearly positive topics need to come toward the start of the overall presentation to provide that initial predisposition toward accepting what the author presents as credible. Such clearly positive topics should also come at
the very end of a presentation, for the last part of an argument the audience
reads will play an important role in creating the final impression that audience has of the overall argument. (Such a final impression can be crucial in

getting an audience to accept an argument once the presentation is completed.)

Topics with a more negative association, however, do not need to be dropped from a presentation entirely. In fact, such topics might be crucial to making a particular point, and their lack of popularity could be related to the reason for which the author is making the overall argument (e.g., trying to change someone's mind on a long-held opinion). Rather, when and how such topics are presented could greatly affect the degree to which an audience reacts to them. (Again, see the discussion of emotional reactions in chapter 1.)

If, for example, an author places all topics with negative associations in the same part of a document (e.g., on the same page), then the author has created a point at which negative audience responses to one topic will be followed by negative responses to the next topic and so on. The result of such an organizational approach could be a loss of author credibility that could result in readers simply abandoning the overall argument and not reading further. In such instances, readers become so negatively predisposed to the topic that they refuse to continue reading.

In other cases, such an organizational structure could cause audiences to become so soured to what they've read that those readers simply dismiss (read but remain negatively predisposed to) the remainder of the author's argument. For this reason, prospective "negative topics" should never be clumped together within a written document. Rather, they should be interspersed with a positive argument/idea both introducing and following such negative topic areas. While such a positive introduction and follow up might not make readers any more receptive to the problematic topic, it prevents an overall loss of reader interest due to the clustering of negative information.

Thus, when organizing a written argument, authors need to ask two additional questions related to topics for which an audience has a negative association:

Which topics might prompt a negative response from my audience?

and

What positive topics should I use to lessen the negative reaction my readers might have to certain topics?

Again, while organizing content into positive-negative-positive blocks will not necessarily prompt a change of heart, it will mitigate the prospective negative reactions of audiences and thus increase the chances that an audience will accept an overall presentation as credible.

16.10 EXTERNALIZING IDEAS: A FINAL PERSPECTIVE

Critical thinking is a process that is internal in nature, for it requires individuals to reflect on and mentally test ideas and opinions. As a result, the only thought process an individual needs to account for when considering ideas is his or her own. Critical writing, by contrast, requires individuals to externalize the results of their thinking. In so doing, they must account for the thought processes of others—namely, the audience with which they share information—if an effective exchange of ideas and opinions is to take place. By using concepts from rhetoric, individuals can begin to think critically not only about ideas but also about the audiences with which they wish to share these ideas. By using a rhetorical framework to ask and answer key questions, the critical thinker can effectively engage others in a wider scale of discourse that prompts all involved parties to think more critically about information and ideas.

BIBLIOGRAPHY

Aristotle. *On Rhetoric*. Translated by George A. Kennedy. New York: Oxford University Press, 1991.
———. *Posterior Analytics*. Translated G. Apostile with commentaries by Hippocrates. Grinnell, Iowa: Peripatetic Press, 1981.
———. *Prior Analytics*. Translated with introduction, notes, and commentary by Robin Smith. Indianapolis: Hackett, 1989.
Bayes, Thomas. *Two Papers by Bayes with Commentaries*. Edited by W. Edwards Deming. 1940. Reprint, New York: Hafner Publishing Company.
Bennett, Jonathan. *A Philosophical Guide to Conditionals*. Oxford University Press, 2003.
Collins, John, Ned Hall, and L.A. Paul, eds. *Counterfactuals and Causation and Counterfactuals*. Cambridge, Mass.: MIT Press, 2004.
Eells, Ellery. *Probabilistic Causality*. Cambridge University Press, 1991.
Flage, Daniel E. *The Art of Questioning: An Introduction to Critical Thinking*. Upper Saddle River, N.J.: Prentice Hall, 2004.
Giere, Ronald N., John Bickle, and Robert F. Maudlin. *Understanding Scientific Reasoning*. Thomson Wadsworth, 2006.
Hacking, Ian. *An Introduction to Probability and Inductive Logic*. Cambridge University Press, 2001.
Hempel, Carl G. *Philosophy of Natural Science* (Foundations of Philosophy). Englewood Cliffs, N.J.: Prentice Hall, 1966.
Jeffrey, Richard. *The Logic of Decision*. Chicago: University of Chicago Press, 1983.
Kvart, Igal. *A Theory of Counterfactuals*. Indianapolis: Hackett, 1986.
Lewis, David. *Counterfactuals*. Basil Blackwell, 1973.

Lipton, Peter. *Inference to Best Explanation*. Routledge, 2004.

Mill, John Stuart. *A System of Logic*. 8th ed. New York: Harper & Brothers, 1895.

Moore, Brooke Noel, and Richard Parker. *Critical Thinking*. 8th ed. Boston: McGraw-Hill, 2007.

Morrow, James D. *Game Theory for Political Scientists*. Princeton, N.J.: Princeton University Press, 1994.

Peirce, Charles Sanders. "Abduction and Induction." In *Philosophical Writings of Peirce*, selected and edited by Justin Buchler. New York: Dover, 1955, 150–56.

Popper, Karl R. *The Logic of Scientific Discovery*. New York: Harper Torchbooks, 1968.

Swinburne, Richard. *An Introduction to Confirmation Theory*. Methuen & Company, 1973.

———. *Epistemic Justification*. Oxford University Press, 2001.

Tetlock, Philip E., and Aaron Belkin. "Counterfactual Thought Experiments in Global Politics: Logical, Methodological, and Psychological Perspectives." In *Counterfactual Thought Experiments in Global Politics: Logical, Methodological, and Psychological Perspectives*, edited by Philip E. Tetlock and Aaron Belkin. Princeton, N.J.: Princeton University Press, 1996, 3–38.

Tetlock, Philip E., and Geoffrey Parker. "Counterfactual History." In *Unmaking the West: "What If?" Scenarios That Rewrite World History*, edited by Philip E. Tetlock, Richard Ned Lebow, and Geoffrey Parker. Ann Arbor: University of Michigan Press, 2006, 363–92.

Venn, John. *Symbolic Logic*. 2nd ed., revised and rewritten. 1894. Reprint, Bronx, N.Y.: Chelsea Publishing Company.

Walton, Douglas. *Ad Hominem Arguments*. Tuscaloosa: University of Alabama Press, 1998.

———. *Appeal to Expert Opinion: Arguments from Authority*. University Park: Pennsylvania State University Press, 1997.

———. *Appeal to Popular Opinion*. University Park: Pennsylvania State University Press, 1999.

Wright, G. H. von. *The Logical Problem of Induction*. 2nd rev. ed. New York: Barnes & Noble, 1965.

Yudkowsky, Eliezer. "An Intuitive Explanation of Bayesian Reasoning." http://yudkowsky.net/bayes/bayes.html. February 22, 2007.

INDEX

abduction, 11, 12n3
absorption, 42, 45
accent, fallacy of, 113
accident, fallacy of, 117
accuracy, 5, 68
affirming the antecedent, 41, 43
affirming the consequent, fallacy of.
    See fallacy of affirming the
    consequent
ambiguity, 1–2, 111–14
ampersand, 40
amphiboly, 112–13
analogical arguments, 7–8, 11n1,
    71–74, 125; analogs, 72; basis, 72;
    criteria (principles) for evaluating,
    73; dissimilarities, 72; diversity of
    analogs, 73; form, 71; inferred
    property, 72; modesty (weakness) of
    conclusion, 73; relevance, 72–73;
    subject, 72
analogs, 72
analogy. *See* analogical arguments
antecedent scenario, 91–92
appeal to authority, 122

appeal to force, 115
appeal to ignorance, 122
appeal to pity, 117
appropriate explanatory content, 76, 80
arguing in a circle. *See* begging the
    question
argument, 6. *See also* distinct kinds of
    arguments
argument reconstruction, 14–15
argumentum ad baculum. See appeal to
    force
argumentum ad hominem. See personal
    attack
argumentum ad misericordiam. See
    appeal to pity
argumentum ad populum. See mob
    appeal
Aristotle, 21, 34
arrow, 41, 48
association, 49, 52
audience response, 157
auxiliary assumptions, 77–78
auxiliary hypotheses. *See* auxiliary
    assumptions

ABOUT THE AUTHORS

Daniel Flage is professor of philosophy at James Madison University. His previous publications have been in critical thinking, logic, and history of modern philosophy.

Noel Hendrickson is assistant professor of philosophy at James Madison University. He has previously published papers in analytic metaphysics and action theory. His current research focuses on counterfactual reasoning and reasoning methods in intelligence analysis.

Kirk St. Amant is associate professor of technical communication and rhetoric at Texas Tech University. His previous publications have focused on intercultural communication, computer-mediated communication, and online education.

William O'Meara is professor of philosophy at James Madison University. His previous publications include coauthoring the James Madison Test in Critical Thinking, editing an introductory reader in philosophy as well as writing articles in American philosophy, phenomenology, and Karl Marx.

William Hawk is professor of philosophy and head of the department of philosophy and religion at James Madison University. His previous publications include articles in ethics and political philosophy specifically having to do with pacifism.